1929

THE
MUSIC MASTER

A LOVE STORY

and

Two Series of Day and Night Songs

by

WILLIAM ALLINGHAM

WITH NINE WOODCUTS

seven designed by ARTHUR HUGHES, *one by* D. G. ROSSETTI, *and one by* JOHN E. MILLAIS, A.R.A.

XEROX

UNIVERSITY MICROFILMS
A Xerox Company

1967

FROM THE EDITOR
TO THE READER

WILLIAM ALLINGHAM, THOUGH KNOWN AS AN IRISH POET and man of letters, was of English family. His father was a bank manager at Bally-shannon in Donegal. There Allingham was born and educated and there he began his literary career. Probably he would be remembered, and deserve to be remembered, if he had written only one poem, the classic nursery song in this book entitled "The Fairies" which begins and ends with the lilting lines:

>   "Up the airy mountain,
>   Down the rushy glen,
>   We daren't go a-hunting
>   For fear of little men;
>   Wee folk, good folk,
>   Trooping all together;
>   Green jacket, red cap,
>   And white owl's feather."

Almost everyone who first encounters this poem wants to memorize it and, in the course of the hundred and twenty years since it was first published, a surprising number of readers, young and old, *have* learned it by heart.

Another striking feature of this book is that it enlisted the skills of three notable artists. Of the nine woodcuts seven were designed by Arthur Hughes, whose illustrations appear in several other books of the Legacy Library, while one is by D. G. Rossetti and the other is by Sir John Millais.

Other books by William Allingham are *Laurence Bloomfield in Ireland* (1864), *Fifty Modern Poems* (1865), *Songs, Poems, and Ballads* (1877), *Evil May Day* (1833), *Blackberries* (1884), *Irish Songs and Poems* (1887), and *The Rambles of Patricius Walker*.

In later years Allingham, who died in 1889, became editor of *Fraser's Magazine* (1874 to 1879), succeeding James Anthony Froude, and among his friends were Leigh Hunt, Carlyle, and Tennyson.

C. A. P.

POEMS.

THE

MUSIC MASTER,

A LOVE STORY,

AND

TWO SERIES OF DAY AND NIGHT SONGS.

BY WILLIAM ALLINGHAM.

WITH NINE WOODCUTS,
SEVEN DESIGNED BY ARTHUR HUGHES, ONE BY D. G. ROSSETTI, AND
ONE BY JOHN E. MILLAIS, A.R.A.

LONDON:
G. ROUTLEDGE & CO. FARRINGDON STREET.
NEW YORK: 18, BEEKMAN STREET.
1855.

TO HIS EXCELLENCY

GEORGE WILLIAM FREDERICK, EARL OF CARLISLE,

K.G., ETC. ETC.

IN WHOM

ANCESTRY, LETTERS, AND PERSONAL WORTH,

COMBINE TO DISTINGUISH

HIS ACCESSION TO THE VICEROYALTY OF IRELAND,

THIS VOLUME

IS, WITH PERMISSION,

VERY RESPECTFULLY INSCRIBED

BY THE AUTHOR.

Militiæ quanquam piger et malus, utilis urbi,
Si das hoc, parvis quoque rebus magna juvari.

HOR. Epis. II. i. 124.

PREFACE.

THIS little volume comprises, along with the *Day and Night Songs* of the writer, published last year, a second series of short poems, and a narrative composition. Some of these appeared in a volume published in 1850 and since withdrawn, some in periodicals; others are now added, and all have been carefully revised. *The Music-Master*, in particular, is perhaps nearly entitled to be considered as a new poem.

Five of the songs or ballads, *The Milkmaid, The Girl's Lamentation, Lovely Mary Donnelly, Nanny's Sailor Lad,* and *The Nobleman's Wedding* have already had an Irish circulation as 'ha'penny ballads,' and the first three were written for this purpose. *The Nobleman's Wedding* is moulded out of a fragmentary ditty sung by an old nurse who was in the family of my respected friend Dr. Petrie, to an air which he intends

to include in his collection of Melodies, now issuing at
intervals from the press for the Society for the Preserva-
tion and Publication of Ancient Irish Music.   Perhaps
I may here remark that I found it not easy, in ballad-
writing, to employ a diction that might hope to come
home to the Irish peasant who speaks English (as most
of them now do), using his customary phraseology, and
also keeping within the laws of poetic taste and the
rules of grammar ; for that phraseology, being as regards
its structural peculiarities but an imperfect or distorted
expression, not an ancient dialect like that of Scotland,
is generally too corrupt (though often forcible) to bear
transplantation into poetry.   Only familiar experience,
too, and constant attention can enable one to use words
in the exact significance which the popular custom has
assigned : for instance, among the Irish peasantry,
" distress," as far as I know, always means *bodily want;*
" trouble," *affliction of mind ;* " misery," *penuriousness;*
" care," *responsibility;* and " sorrow" commonly means
ill-luck, misfortune ; while " sorry" has the usual dic-

tionary meaning. From these conditions it comes that the choice of words for poetry in Irish-English is narrowly limited, instead of there being that accession both of variety and raciness which is sometimes in the gift of a genuine peculiar dialect.

Those excellent painters who on my behalf have submitted their genius to the risks of wood-engraving will, I hope, pardon me for placing a word of sincere thanks in the book they have honoured with this evidence, through art, of their valued friendship.

As to the book itself, which belongs to the period of youth and early manhood, I can unaffectedly say I spend little thought, and make less claim, with regard to its chances of reception ; satisfied with its being a genuine poetic result, however small a one, of my experience thus far. There are at least some who will receive it kindly, for whose sake it is worth while to publish it, and to plan future pages that may better deserve their perusal.

W. A.

Ballyshannon, Ireland, May 1855.

Through harmony of words may murmur the harmony of things; whispers of human life and the world our scene, pensive memories and high hopes musically mingling. These, at fit moments, may soothe, cheer, strengthen.

CONTENTS.

CONTENTS.

WOODCUTS.

Engraved by Dalziel.

DAY AND NIGHT SONGS.

First Series.

1.

THE VALLEY STREAM.

STREAM flowing swiftly, what music is thine!
The breezy rock-pass, and the storm-wooing pine,

    Have taught thee their murmurs,

    Their wild mountain murmurs;

Subdued in thy liquid response to a sound
Which aids the repose of this pastoral ground;
Where our valley yet mingles an awe with the love
It smiles to the sheltering bastions above;—

    Thy cloud-haunted birthplace,

    O Stream, flowing swiftly!

Encircle our meadows with bounty and grace;
Then move on thy journey with tranquiller pace,

    To find the great waters,

    The great ocean-waters,

Blue, wonderful, boundless to vision or thought ;—
Thence, thence, might thy musical tidings be brought!
One waft of the tones of the infinite sea!
Our gain is but songs of the mountain from thee :

      Thy primitive issue,
      Thou Stream of our valley !

And have we divined what is thunder'd and hiss'd,
Where the awful ledge glimmers through screens of
    grey mist,

      And raves forth its secrets,
      The heart of its secrets ?
Or learn'd what is hid in thy whispering note,
Mysteriously gather'd from fountains remote,
Where the solitudes spread in the upper sunshine ?
O Stream flowing swiftly, what music is thine ?

      Far-wafted, prophetic ?
      Thou Stream of our valley !

II.

EVEY.

Bud and leaflet, opening slowly,
    Woo'd with tears by winds of Spring,
Now, of June persuaded wholly,
    Perfumes, flow'rs, and shadows bring.

Evey, in the linden alley,
    All alone I met to-day,
Tripping to the sunny valley
    Spread across with new-mown hay.

Brown her soft curls, sunbeam-sainted,
    Golden in the wavering flush ;
Darker brown her eyes are, painted
    Eye and fringe with one soft brush.

Through the leaves a careless comer,
  Never nymph of fount or tree
Could have press'd the floor of summer
  With a lighter foot than she.

Can this broad hat, fasten'd under
  With a bright blue ribbon's flow,
Change my pet so much, I wonder,
  Of a month or two ago?

Half too changed to speak I thought her,
  Till the pictured silence broke,
Sweet and clear as dropping water,
  Into words she sung or spoke.

Few her words; yet, like a sister,
  Trustfully she look'd and smiled;
'Twas but in my soul I kiss'd her
  As I used to kiss the child.

Shadows, which are not of sadness,
  Touch her eyes, and brow above.
As pale wild roses dream of redness,
  Dreams her innocent heart of love.

————————

III.

WINDLASS SONG.

HEAVE at the windlass!—Heave O, cheerly, men!
Heave all at once, with a will!
The tide's quickly making,
Our cordage is creaking,
The water has put on a frill,
Heave O!

Fare you well, sweethearts!—Heave O, cheerly, men!
Shore gambarado and sport!
The good ship all ready,
Each dog-vane is steady,
The wind blowing dead out of port,
Heave O!

Once in blue water—Heave O, cheerly, men!

    Blow it from north or from south;

       She'll stand to it tightly,

       And curtsey politely,

    And carry a bone in her mouth,

              Heave O!

Short cruise or long cruise—Heave O, cheerly, men!

    Jolly Jack Tar thinks it one.

       No latitude dreads he

       Of White, Black, or Red Sea,

    Great ice-bergs, or tropical sun,

              Heave O!

One other turn, and Heave O, cheerly, men!

    Heave, and good-bye to the shore!

       Our money, how went it?

       We shared it and spent it;

    Next year we'll come back with some more,

              Heave O!

IV.

VENUS OF THE NEEDLE.

O MARYANNE, you pretty girl,
   Intent on silky labour,
Of sempstresses the pink and pearl,
   Excuse a peeping neighbour!

Those eyes, for ever drooping, give
   The long brown lashes rarely ;
But violets in the shadows live,—
   For once unveil them fairly.

Hast thou not lent that flounce enough
   Of looks so long and earnest ?
Lo, here's more " penetrable stuff,"
   To which thou never turnest.

Ye graceful fingers, deftly sped!
  How slender, and how nimble!
O might I wind their skeins of thread,
  Or but pick up their thimble!

How blest the youth whom love shall bring,
  And happy stars embolden,
To change the dome into a ring,
  The silver into golden!

Who'll steal some morning to her side
  To take her finger's measure,
While Maryanne pretends to chide,
  And blushes deep with pleasure.

Who'll watch her sew her wedding-gown,
  Well conscious that it *is* hers ;
Who'll glean a tress, without a frown,
  With those so ready scissors.

Who'll taste those ripenings of the south,
　　The fragrant and delicious—
Don't put the pins into your mouth,
　　O Maryanne, my precious!

I almost wish it were my trust
　　To teach how shocking that is;
I wish I had not, as I must,
　　To quit this tempting lattice.

Sure aim takes Cupid, fluttering foe,
　　Across a street so narrow;
A thread of silk to string his bow,
　　A needle for his arrow!

V.

THE FISHERMAN.

BY GOETHE.

THE water gush'd, the water swell'd;
  A Fisherman thereby
Sat gazing on the line he held,
  With tranquil heart and eye;
And as he look'd, and as he loll'd,
  The parting water surged;
And, rustling from the wave that roll'd,
  A Woman's form emerged.

She sung to him, she spake to him:
  "Why lure my brood away,
By human skill, and human fraud,
  Up to the burning day?

Oh, happy live the little fish !
   So happy—mightst thou know,
This moment 'twere thine only wish
   To come to us below.

" Finds not the Sun a resting-place ;
   The Moon, within the mere ?
Uplifts not each a radiant face,
   Grown doubly bright and clear ?
Persuade thee not these heav'ns so deep ?
   This moist, embracing blue ?
Thy features, lo ! that swim and sleep
   In soft eternal dew ?"

The water gush'd, the water swell'd,
   It kiss'd his naked feet ;
Deep longing all his heart impell'd,
   As when our love we meet.
She spake to him, she sung to him ;
   No help could come between ;
Half drew she him, half sank he in,
   And never more was seen.

VI.

ÆOLIAN HARP.

WHAT saith the river to the rushes grey,
    Rushes sadly bending,
    River slowly wending?
Who can tell the whisper'd things they say?
    Youth, and prime, and life, and time,
    For ever, ever fled away!

Drop your wither'd garlands in the stream,
    Low autumnal branches,
    Round the skiff that launches
Wavering downward through the lands of dream.
    Ever, ever fled away!
    This the burden, this the theme.

What saith the river to the rushes grey,
    Rushes sadly bending,
    River slowly wending ?
It is near the closing of the day.
    Near the night.   Life and light
    For ever, ever fled away !

Draw him tideward down ; but not in haste.
    Mouldering daylight lingers ;
    Night with her cold fingers
Sprinkles moonbeams on the dim sea-waste.
    Ever, ever fled away !
    Vainly cherish'd ! vainly chased !

What saith the river to the rushes grey,
    Rushes sadly bending,
    River slowly wending ?
Where in darkest glooms his bed we lay,
    Up the cave moans the wave,
    For ever, ever, ever fled away !

VII.

OH! WERE MY LOVE.

OH! were my Love a country lass,
　　That I might see her every day;
And sit with her on hedgerow grass
　　Beneath a bough of May;
And find her cattle when astray,
　　Or help to drive them to the field,
And linger on our homeward way,
　　And woo her lips to yield
A twilight kiss before we parted,
Full of love, yet easy-hearted.

Oh! were my Love a cottage maid,
　　To spin through many a winter night,
Where ingle-corner lends its shade
　　From fir-wood blazing bright.

C

Beside her wheel what dear delight
    To watch the blushes go and come
With tender words, that took no fright
    Beneath the friendly hum;
Or rising smile, or tear-drop swelling,
At a fireside legend's telling.

Oh! were my Love a peasant girl,
    That never saw the wicked town;
Was never dight with silk or pearl,
    But graced a homely gown.
How less than weak were fashion's frown
    To vex our unambitious lot;
How rich were love and peace to crown
    Our green secluded cot;
Where Age would come serene and shining,
Like an autumn day's declining!

VIII.

THE FAIRIES.

A NURSERY SONG.

UP the airy mountain,
    Down the rushy glen,
We daren't go a hunting
    For fear of little men;
Wee folk, good folk,
    Trooping all together;
Green jacket, red cap,
    And white owl's feather!

Down along the rocky shore
    Some make their home,
They live on crispy pancakes
    Of yellow tide-foam;

c 2

Some in the reeds
    Of the black mountain-lake,
With frogs for their watch-dogs,
    All night awake.

High on the hill-top
    The. old King sits;
He is now so old and grey
    He's nigh lost his wits.
With a bridge of white mist
    Columbkill he crosses,
On his stately journeys
    From Slieveleague to Rosses;
Or going up with music
    On cold starry nights,
To sup with the Queen
    Of the gay Northern Lights.

They stole little Bridget
    For seven years long;
When she came down again
    Her friends were all gone.

They took her lightly back,
  Between the night and morrow,
They thought that she was fast asleep,
  But she was dead with sorrow.
They have kept her ever since
  Deep within the lakes,
On a bed of flag-leaves,
  Watching till she wakes.

By the craggy hill-side,
  Through the mosses bare,
They have planted thorn-trees
  For pleasure here and there.
Is any man so daring
  To dig one up in spite,
He shall find the thornies set
  In his bed at night.

Up the airy mountain,
  Down the rushy glen,
We daren't go a hunting
  For fear of little men ;

Wee folk, good folk,
  Trooping all together;
Green jacket, red cap,
  And white owl's feather!

————————

IX.

THE RUINED CHAPEL.

By the shore, a plot of ground
Clips a ruin'd chapel round,
Buttress'd with a grassy mound;
  Where Day and Night and Day go by,
And bring no touch of human sound.

Washing of the lonely seas,
Shaking of the guardian trees,
Piping of the salted breeze;
  Day and Night and Day go by
To the endless tune of these.

Or when, as winds and waters keep
A hush more dead than any sleep,
Still morns to stiller evenings creep,
   And Day and Night and Day go by;
Here the silence is most deep.

The empty ruins, lapsed again
Into Nature's wide domain,
Sow themselves with seed and grain
   As Day and Night and Day go by;
And hoard June's sun and April's rain.

Here fresh funeral tears were shed;
And now the graves are also dead;
And suckers from the ash-tree spread,
   While Day and Night and Day go by;
And stars move calmly overhead.

————————

X

A DREAM.

I HEARD the dogs howl in the moonlight night,
And I went to the window to see the sight;
All the dead that ever I knew
Going one by one and two by two.

On they pass'd, and on they pass'd;
Townsfellows all from first to last;
Born in the moonlight of the lane,
And quench'd in the heavy shadow again.

Schoolmates, marching as when we play'd
At soldiers once—but now more staid;
Those were the strangest sight to me
Who were drown'd, I knew, in the awful sea.

Straight and handsome folk ; bent and weak too ;
And some that I loved, and gasp'd to speak to ;
Some but a day in their churchyard bed ;
And some that I had not known were dead.

A long, long crowd—where each seem'd lonely.
And yet of them all there was one, one only,
That rais'd a head, or look'd my way ;
And she seem'd to linger, but might not stay.

How long since I saw that fair pale face !
Ah, mother dear, might I only place
My head on thy breast, a moment to rest,
While thy hand on my tearful cheek were prest !

On, on, a moving bridge they made
Across the moon-stream, from shade to shade
Young and old, women and men ;
Many long-forgot, but remember'd then.

And first there came a bitter laughter;

And a sound of tears a moment after;

And then a music so lofty and gay,

That every morning, day by day,

I strive to recall it if I may.

XI.

"LEVAVI OCULOS."

I CRIED to God, in trouble for my sin ;
To the Great God who dwelleth in the deeps.
The deeps return not any voice or sign.

But with my soul I know thee, O Great God ;
The soul thou givest knoweth thee, Great God ;
And with my soul I sorrow for my sin.

Full sure I am there is no joy in sin,
Joy-scented Peace is trampled under foot,
Like a white growing blossom into mud.

Sin is establish'd subtly in the heart
As a disease ; like a magician foul
Ruleth the better thoughts against their will.

Only the rays of God can cure the heart,
Purge it of evil: there's no other way
Except to turn with the whole heart to God.

In heavenly sunlight live no shades of fear ;
The soul there, busy or at rest, hath peace ;
And music floweth from the various world.

The Lord is great and good, and is our God.
There needeth not a word but only these ;
Our God is good, our God is great.   'Tis well.

All things are ever God's ; the shows of things
Are of men's fantasy, and warp'd with sin ;
God, and the things of God, immutable.

O great good God, my pray'r is to neglect
The shows of fantasy, and turn myself
To thy unfenced, unbounded warmth and light !

Then were all shows of things a part of truth :
Then were my soul, if busy or at rest,
Residing in the house of perfect peace !

XII.

CROSS-EXAMINATION.

WHAT knowest thou of this eternal code?
  As much as God intended to display.

Wilt thou affirm thou knowest aught of God?
  Nor save his works, that creature ever may.

Is not thy life at times a weary load?
  Which aimless on my back he would not lay.

Is it all good thy conscience doth forebode?
  The deepest thought doth least my soul affray.

When hath a glimpse of Heav'n been ever show'd?
  Whilst walking straight, I never miss its ray.

Why should such destiny to thee be owed?
  Easy alike to him are yea and nay.

Why shouldst thou reach it by so mean a road ?
  Ask that of him who set us in the way.

Art thou more living than a finch or toad ?
  Is soul sheer waste, if we be such as they ?

Thou never wilt prevail to loose the node.
  If so, 'twere loss of labour to essay.

Nor to uproot these doubts so thickly sow'd.
  Nor thou these deeplier-rooted hopes to slay.

XIII.

THE CUPIDS.

I.

In a grove I saw one day
A flight of Cupids all at play,
Flitting bird-like through the air,
Or alighting here and there,
Making every bough rejoice
With a most celestial voice,
Or amongst the blossoms found
Rolling on the swarded ground.
Some there were with wings of blue,
Other some, of rosy hue,
Here, one plumed with purest white,
There, as dyed in golden light;

Crimson some, and some I saw
Colour'd like a gay macaw.
Many were the Queen of Beauty's—
Many bound to other duties.

II.

A band of fowlers next I spied,
Spreading nets on every side,
Watching long, by skill or hap
Fleeting Cupids to entrap.
But if one at length was ta'en,
After mickle time and pain,
Whether golden one or blue,
Piebald, or of rosy hue,
When they put him in their cage
He grew meagre as with age,
Plumage rumpled, colour coarse,
Voice unfrequent, sad, and hoarse;
And little pleasure had they in him
Who had spent the day to win him.

D

XIV

LOVELY MARY DONNELLY.

(*To an Irish Tune.*)

Oʜ, lovely Mary Donnelly, it's you I love the best!

If fifty girls were round you I'd hardly see the rest.

Be what it may the time of day, the place be where
it will,

Sweet looks of Mary Donnelly, they bloom before me
still.

Her eyes like mountain water that's flowing on a rock,

How clear they are, how dark they are! and they give
me many a shock.

Red rowans warm in sunshine and wetted with a
show'r,

Could ne'er express the charming lip that has me in
its pow'r.

Her nose is straight and handsome, her eyebrows
 lifted up,
Her chin is very neat and pert, and smooth like a
 china cup,
Her hair's the brag of Ireland, so weighty and so fine ;
It's rolling down upon her neck, and gather'd in a twine.

The dance o' last Whit-Monday night exceeded all before,
No pretty girl for miles about was missing from the
 floor ;
But Mary kept the belt of love, and O but she was gay !
She danced a jig, she sung a song, that took my heart
 away.

When she stood up for dancing, her steps were so
 complete,
The music nearly kill'd itself to listen to her feet ;
The fiddler moan'd his blindness, he heard her so much
 praised,
But bless'd himself he wasn't deaf when once her
 voice she raised.

And evermore I'm whistling or lilting what you sung,

Your smile is always in my heart, your name beside
my tongue;

But you've as many sweethearts as you'd count on
both your hands,

And for myself there's not a thumb or little finger
stands.

Oh, you're the flower o' womankind in country or in
town;

The higher I exalt you, the lower I'm cast down.

If some great lord should come this way, and see your
beauty bright,

And you to be his lady, I'd own it was but right.

O might we live together in a lofty palace hall,

Where joyful music rises, and where scarlet curtains
fall!

O might we live together in a cottage mean and small;

With sods of grass the only roof, and mud the only
wall!

O lovely Mary Donnelly, your beauty's my distress.

It's far too beauteous to be mine, but I'll never wish
it less.

The proudest place would fit your face, and I am poor
and low;

But blessings be about you, dear, wherever you may go!

XV.

SONNET.

IN A SPRING GROVE.

HERE the white-ray'd anemone is born,
Wood-sorrel, and the varnish'd buttercup ;
And primrose in its purfled green swathed up,
Pallid and sweet round every budding thorn,
Grey ash, and beech with rusty leaves outworn.
Here, too, the darting linnet has her nest
In the blue-lustred holly, never shorn,
Whose partner cheers her little brooding breast,
Piping from some near bough.   O simple song !
O cistern deep of that harmonious rillet,
And these fair juicy stems that climb and throng
The vernal world, and unexhausted seas
Of flowing life, and soul that asks to fill it,
Each and all these,—and more, and more than these !

XVI.

SERENADE.

Oh, hearing sleep, and sleeping hear,
The while we dare to call thee dear,
So may thy dreams be good, although
The loving power thou canst not know!
As music parts the silence, lo!
Through heav'n the stars begin to peep,
To comfort us that darkling pine
Because those fairer lights of thine
Have set into the Sea of Sleep.
Yet closèd still thine eyelids keep;
And may our voices through the sphere
Of Dreamland all as softly rise
As through these shadowy rural dells,
Where bashful Echo sleeping dwells,

And touch thy spirit to as soft replies.
And peace from gentle guardian skies,
Till watches of the dark be worn,
Surround thy bed,—and joyous morn
Makes all the chamber rosy bright!
Good-night!—From far-off fields is borne
The drowsy Echo's faint " Good-night,"—
Good-night!   Good-night!

———————

XVII.

THE DIRTY OLD MAN

A LAY OF LEADENHALL.

In a dirty old house lived a Dirty Old Man ;
Soap, towels, or brushes were not in his plan.
For forty long years, as the neighbours declared,
His house never once had been clean'd or repair'd.

'Twas a scandal and shame to the business-like street,
One terrible blot in a ledger so neat :
The shop full of hardware, but black as a hearse,
And the rest of the mansion a thousand times worse.

Outside, the old plaster, all spatter and stain,
Looked spotty in sunshine and streaky in rain ;
The window-sills sprouted with mildewy grass,
And the panes from being broken were known to be
    glass.

On the ricketty signboard no learning could spell
The merchant who sold, or the goods he'd to sell;
But for house and for man a new title took growth,
Like a fungus,—the Dirt gave its name to them both.

Within, there were carpets and cushions of dust,
The wood was half rot, and the metal half rust,
Old curtains—half cobwebs—hung grimly aloof;
'Twas a Spiders' Elysium from cellar to roof.

There, king of the spiders, the Dirty Old Man
Lives busy and dirty as ever he can;
With dirt on his fingers and dirt on his face,
For the Dirty Old Man thinks the dirt no disgrace.

From his wig to his shoes, from his coat to his shirt,
His clothes are a proverb, a marvel of dirt;
The dirt is pervading, unfading, exceeding,—
Yet the Dirty Old Man has both learning and
    breeding.

Fine dames from their carriages, noble and fair,
Have entered his shop—less to buy than to stare;
And have afterwards said, though the dirt was so
    frightful,
The Dirty Man's manners were truly delightful.

But they pried not upstairs, through the dirt and the
    gloom,
Nor peep'd at the door of the wonderful room
That gossips made much of, in accents subdued,
But whose inside no mortal might boast to have
    view'd.

That room — forty years since, folk settled and
    deck'd it.
The luncheon's prepared, and the guests are expected.
The handsome young host he is gallant and gay,
For his love and her friends will be with him
    to-day.

With solid and dainty the table is drest,

The wine beams its brightest, the flowers bloom their
        best ;

Yet the host need not smile, and no guests will appear,

For his sweetheart is dead, as he shortly shall hear.

Full forty years since, turn'd the key in that door.

'Tis a room deaf and dumb 'mid the city's uproar.

The guests, for whose joyance that table was spread,

May now enter as ghosts, for they're every one dead.

Through a chink in the shutter dim lights come and go ;

The seats are in order, the dishes a-row ;

But the luncheon was wealth to the rat and the mouse

Whose descendants have long left the Dirty Old House.

Cup and platter are mask'd in thick layers of dust ;

The flowers fall'n to powder, the wine swath'd in crust ;

A nosegay was laid before one special chair,

And the faded blue ribbon that bound it lies there.

The old man has play'd out his parts in the scene.

Wherever he now is, I hope he's more clean.

Yet give we a thought free of scoffing or ban

To that Dirty Old House and that Dirty Old Man.

[A singular man, named Nathaniel Bentley, for many years
kept a large hardware shop in Leadenhall-street, London. He
was best known as Dirty Dick (Dick, for alliteration's sake,
probably), and his place of business as the Dirty Warehouse. He
died about the year 1809. These verses accord with the accounts
respecting himself and his house.]

XVIII.

THE BRIGHT LITTLE GIRL.

(To an Irish Tune.)

HER blue eyes they beam and they twinkle,
　　Her lips have made smiling more fair ;
On cheek and on brow there's no wrinkle,
　　But thousands of curls in her hair.

She's little,—you don't wish her taller ;
　　Just half through the teens is her age ;
And baby or lady to call her,
　　Were something to puzzle a sage !

Her walk is far better than dancing ;
　　She speaks as another might sing ;
And all by an innocent chancing,
　　Like lambkins and birds in the spring.

Unskill'd in the airs of the city,
   She's perfect in natural grace;
She's gentle, and truthful, and witty,
   And ne'er spends a thought on her face.

Her face, with the fine glow that's in it,
   As fresh as an apple-tree bloom—
And O! when she comes, in a minute,
   Like sunbeams she brightens the room.

As taking in mind as in feature,
   How many will sigh for her sake!
—I wonder, the sweet little creature,
   What sort of a wife she would make.

XIX.

THE WAYSIDE WELL.

O THOU pretty Wayside Well,
 Wreath'd about with roses !
Where, beguiled with soothing spell,
 Weary foot reposes.

With a welcome fresh and green
 Wave thy border grasses,
By the dusty traveller seen,
 Sighing as he passes.

Cup of no Circean bliss,
 Charity of summer,
Making happy with a kiss
 Every meanest comer !

Morning, too, and eventide,
   Without stint or measure,
Cottage households near and wide
   Share thy liquid treasure.

Fair the greeting face ascends,
   Like a naiad daughter,
When the peasant lassie bends
   To thy trembling water.

When a laddie brings her pail
   Down the twilight meadow,
Tender falls the whisper'd tale,
   Soft the double shadow !

Clear as childhood in thy look,
   Nature seems to pet thee ;
Fierce July that drains the brook
   Hath no power to fret thee.

Shelter'd cool and free from smirch
    In thy cavelet shady,
O'er thee in a silver birch
    Stoops a forest lady.

To thy glass the Star of Eve
    Shyly dares to bend her;
Matron Moon thy depths receive,
    Globed in mellow splendour.

Bounteous Spring! for ever own
    Undisturb'd thy station;
Not to thirsty lips alone
    Serving mild donation.

Never come the newt or frog,
    Pebble thrown in malice,
Mud or wither'd leaves, to clog
    Or defile thy chalice.

Heaven be still within thy ken,
    Through the veil thou wearest,—
Glimpsing clearest, as with men,
    When the boughs are barest!

THE LOVER AND BIRDS.

WITHIN a budding grove,

In April's ear sang every bird his best,

But not a song to pleasure my unrest,

Or touch the tears unwept of bitter love.

Some spake, methought, with pity, some as if in jest.

To every word

Of every bird

I listen'd, and replied as it behove.

Scream'd Chaffinch, "Sweet, sweet, sweet!

O bring my pretty love to meet me here!"

"Chaffinch," quoth I, "be dumb awhile, in fear

Thy darling prove no better than a cheat;

And never come, or fly when wintry days appear."

Yet from a twig

With voice so big,

The little fowl his utterance did repeat.

Then I, "the man forlorn

Hears Earth send up a foolish noise aloft."

"And what'll *he* do? what'll *he* do!" scoff'd

The Blackbird, standing in an ancient thorn,

Then spread his sooty wings and flitted to the croft,

         With cackling laugh:

         Whom I, being half

Enraged, call'd after, giving back his scorn.

  Worse mock'd the Thrush, "Die! die!

O could he do it? could he do it?   Nay!

Be quick! be quick!   Here, here, here!" (went his
    lay)

"Take heed! take heed!" then, "Why? why? why?
    why? why?

See—ee now! see—ee now!" (he drawl'd) "Back! back!
    back!   R-r-r-run away!"

         O Thrush, be still!

         Or, at thy will,

Seek some less sad interpreter than I!

" Air, air! blue air and white!

Whither I flee, whither, O whither, O whither I
    flee!"

(Thus the Lark hurried, mounting from the lea)

" Hills, countries, many waters glittering bright,

Whither I see, whither I see! deeper, deeper, deeper,
    whither I see, see, see!"

        Gay Lark, I said,

        The song that's bred

In happy nest may well to heav'n make flight.

    " There's something, something sad,

I half remember"—piped a broken strain.

Well sung, sweet Robin!   Robin sung again,

" Spring's opening cheerily, cheerily! be we glad!"

Which moved, I wist not why, me melancholy mad,

        Till now, grown meek,

        With wetted cheek,

Most comforting and gentle thoughts I had.

XXI.

THE MILKMAID.

(To the tune of " *It was an old Beggarman.*")

O, WHERE are you going so early ? he said ;
Good luck go with you, my pretty maid ;
To tell you my mind I'm half afraid,
   But I wish I were your sweetheart.
      When the morning sun is shining low,
      And the cocks in every farmyard crow,
        I'll carry your pail,
        O'er hill and dale,
      And I'll go with you a-milking.

I'm going a-milking, sir, says she,
Through the dew, and across the lea ;
You ne'er would even yourself to me,
   Or take me for your sweetheart.
      When the morning sun, &c.

Now give me your milking stool awhile,
To carry it down to yonder stile ;
I'm wishing every step a mile,
　　And myself your only sweetheart.
　　　　When the morning sun, &c.

O, here's the stile in-under the tree,
And there's the path in the grass for me,
And I thank you kindly, sir, says she,
　　And wish you a better sweetheart.
　　　　When the morning sun, &c.

Now give me your milking-pail, says he,
And while we're going across the lea,
Pray reckon your master's cows to me,
　　Although I'm not your sweetheart.
　　　　When the morning sun, &c.

Two of them red, and two of them white,
Two of them yellow and silky bright,
She told him her master's cows aright.
　　Though he was not her sweetheart.
　　　　When the morning sun, &c.

She sat and milk'd in the morning sun,

And when her milking was over and done,

She found him waiting, all as one

 As if he were her sweetheart.

   When the morning sun, &c.

He freely offer'd his heart and hand;

Now she has a farm at her command,

And cows of her own to graze the land;

 Success to all true sweethearts!

   When the morning sun is shining low,

   And the cocks in every farmyard crow,

    I'll carry your pail

    O'er hill and dale,

   And I'll go with you a-milking.

XXII.

THE LIGHTHOUSE.

THE plunging storm flies fierce against the pane,
    And thrills our cottage with redoubled shocks;
The chimney mutters and the rafters strain;
    Without, the breakers roar along the rocks.

See, from our fire and taper-lighted room,
    How savage, pitiless, and uncontroll'd
The grim horizon shows its tossing gloom
    Of waves from unknown angry gulphs uproll'd;

Where, underneath that black portentous lid,
    A long pale space between the night and sea
Gleams awful; while in deepest darkness hid
    All other things in our despair agree.

But lo ! what star amid the thickest dark
  A soft and unexpected dawn has made ?
O welcome Lighthouse, thy unruffled spark,
  Piercing the turmoil and the deathly shade !

By such a glimpse o'er the distracted wave
  Full many a soul to-night is re-possest
Of courage and of order, strong to save ;
  And like effect it works within my breast.

Three faithful men have set themselves to stand
  Against all storms that from the sky can blow,
Where peril must expect no aiding hand,
  And tedium no relief may hope to know.

Nor shout they, passing brothers to inform
  What weariness they feel, or what affright ;
But tranquilly in solitude and storm
  Abide from month to month, and show their light.

XXIII

THE TOUCHSTONE.

A MAN there came, whence none could tell,
　　Bearing a Touchstone in his hand;
　　And tested all things in the land
By its unerring spell.

Quick birth of transmutation smote
　　The fair to foul, the foul to fair;
　　Purple nor ermine did he spare,
Nor scorn the dusty coat.

Of heir-loom jewels, prized so much,
　　Were many changed to chips and clods,
　　And even statues of the Gods
Crumbled beneath its touch.

Then angrily the people cried,
    " The loss outweighs the profit far;
    Our goods suffice us as they are;
We will not have them tried."

And since they could not so avail
    To check his unrelenting quest,
    They seized him, saying—" Let him test
How real is our jail!"

But, though they slew him with the sword,
    And in a fire his Touchstone burn'd,
    Its doings could not be o'erturn'd,
Its undoings restored.

And when, to stop all future harm,
    They strew'd its ashes on the breeze;
    They little guess'd each grain of these
Convey'd the perfect charm.

XXIV.

ÆOLIAN HARP.

Is it all in vain?
Strangely throbbing pain,
Trembling joy of memory!
Bygone things, how shadowy
Within their graves they lie!

Shall I sit then by their graves,
Listening to the melancholy waves?
I would fain.
But even these in vapours die:
For nothing may remain.

One survivor in a boat
On the wide dim deep afloat,
When the sunken ship is gone,
Lit by late stars before the dawn.

The sea rolls vaguely, and the stars are dumb.

 The ship is sunk full many a year.

  Dream no more of loss or gain :

 A ship was never here.

A dawn will never, never come.

  —Is it all in vain ?

————————

LADY ALICE.

I.

Now what doth Lady Alice so late on the turret stair,

Without a lamp to light her, but the diamond in her hair;

When every arching passage overflows with shallow
gloom,

And dreams float through the castle, into every silent
room?

She trembles at her footsteps, although they fall so
light;

Through the turret loopholes she sees the wild midnight;

Broken vapours streaming across the stormy sky;

Down the empty corridors the blast doth moan and cry.

She steals along a gallery; she pauses by a door;

And fast her tears are dropping down upon the oaken
floor;

And thrice she seems returning—but thrice she turns
    again :—

Now heavy lie the cloud of sleep on that old father's
    brain !

Oh, well it were that *never* shouldst thou waken from
    thy sleep!

For wherefore should they waken, who waken but to
    weep ?

No more, no more beside thy bed doth Peace a vigil keep,

But Woe,—a lion that awaits thy rousing for its leap.

II.

An afternoon of April, no sun appears on high,

But a moist and yellow lustre fills the deepness of the sky:

And through the castle-gateway, left empty and forlorn,

Along the leafless avenue an honour'd bier is borne.

They stop.   The long line closes up like some gigantic
    worm ;

A shape is standing in the path, a wan and ghost-like
    form,

F

Which gazes fixedly ; nor moves, nor utters any sound ;
Then, like a statue built of snow, sinks down upon the
    ground.

And though her clothes are ragged, and though her
    feet are bare,
And though all wild and tangled falls her heavy silk-
    brown hair ;
Though from her eyes the brightness, from her cheeks
    the bloom is fled,
They know their Lady Alice, the darling of the dead.

With silence, in her own old room the fainting form
    they lay,
Where all things stand unalter'd since the night she
    fled away :
But who—but who shall bring to life her father from
    the clay ?
But who shall give her back again her heart of a former
    day ?

XXVI.

THERANIA.

O Unknown Belov'd One! to the mellow season
    Branches in the lawn make drooping bow'rs;
  Vase and plot burn scarlet, gold, and azure;
  Honeysuckles wind the tall grey turret,
      And pale passion-flow'rs.
  Come thou, come thou to my lonely thought,
          O Unknown Belov'd One.

Now, at evening twilight, dusky dew down-wavers,
    Soft stars crown the grove-encircled hill;
  Breathe the new-mown meadows, broad and misty;
  Through the heavy grass the rail is talking;
      All beside is still.
  Trace with me the wandering avenue,
          O Unknown Belov'd One.

In the mystic realm, and in the time of visions,

    I thy lover have no need to woo ;

   There I hold thy hand in mine, thou dearest,

   And thy soul in mine, and feel its throbbing,

    Tender, deep, and true :

   Then my tears are love, and thine are love,

    O Unknown Belov'd One !

Is thy voice a wavelet on the listening darkness ?

    Are thine eyes unfolding from their veil ?

   Wilt thou come before the signs of winter—

   Days that shred the bough with trembling fingers,

    Nights that weep and wail ?

   Art thou Love indeed, or art thou Death,

    O Unknown Belov'd One ?

XXVII.

WAYCONNELL TOWER.

THE tangling wealth by June amass'd,
  Left rock and ruin vaguely seen;
Thick ivy-cables held them fast,
  Light boughs descended, floating green.

Slow turn'd the stair, a breathless height,
  And, far above, it set me free,
When all the golden fan of light
  Was closing down into the sea.

A window half-way up the wall
  It led to; and so high was that,
The tallest trees were not so tall
  That they could reach to where I sat.

Aloft within the moulder'd tower,
　　Dark ivy fringed its round of sky,
Where slowly, in the deepening hour,
　　The first faint stars unveil'd on high.

The rustling of the foliage dim,
　　The murmur of the cool grey tide,
With tears that trembled on the brim,
　　An echo sad to these I sigh'd.

O Sea, thy ripple's mournful tune!—
　　The cloud along the sunset sleeps;
The phantom of the golden moon
　　Is kindled in thy quivering deeps,

Oh, mournfully!—and I to fill,
　　Fix'd in a ruin-window strange,
Some countless period, watching still
　　A moon, a sea, that never change!

The guided orb is mounting slow ;
   The duteous wave is ebbing fast ;
And now, as from the niche I go,
   A shadow joins the shadowy past.

Farewell ! dim ruins ; tower and life ;
   Sadly enrich the distant view !
And welcome, scenes of toil and strife ;
   To-morrow's sun arises new.

XXVIII.

THE WITCH-BRIDE.

A FAIR witch crept to a young man's side,
And he kiss'd her and took her for his bride.

But a Shape came in at the dead of night,
And fill'd the room with snowy light.

And he saw how in his arms there lay
A thing more frightful than mouth may say.

And he rose in haste, and follow'd the Shape
Till morning crown'd an eastern cape.

And he girded himself and follow'd still,
When sunset sainted the western hill.

But, mocking and thwarting, clung to his side,
Weary day!—the foul Witch-Bride.

XXIX.

SPRING IS COME.

Ye coax the timid verdure
 Along the hills of Spring,
Blue skies and gentle breezes,
 And soft clouds wandering !
The quire of birds on budding spray,
 Loud larks in ether sing;
A fresher pulse, a wider day,
 Give joy to everything.

The gay translucent morning
 Lies glittering on the sea,
The noonday sprinkles shadows
 Athwart the daisied lea;

The round Sun's sinking scarlet rim
   In vapour hideth he,
The darkling hours are cool and dim,
   As vernal night should be.

Our Earth has not grown aged,
   With all her countless years ;
She works, and never wearies,
   Is glad, and nothing fears :
The glow of air, broad land and wave,
   In season re-appears ;
And shall, when slumber in the grave
   These human smiles and tears.

Oh, rich in songs and colours,
   Thou joy-reviving Spring !
Some hopes are chill'd with winter
   Whose term thou canst not bring.
Some voices answer not thy call
   When sky and woodland ring,
Some faces come not back at all
   With primrose-blossoming.

The distant-flying swallow,
　The upward-yearning seed,
Find nature's promise faithful,
　Attain their humble meed.
Great Parent! thou hast also form'd
　These hearts which throb and bleed;
With love, truth, hope, their life hast warm'd,
　And what is best, decreed.

XXX.

THE MESSENGER.

A MESSENGER, that stood beside my bed,
In words of clear and cruel import said,
(And yet methought the tone was less unkind,)
" I bring thee pain of body and of mind."

" Each gift of each must pay a toll to me ;
Nor flight, nor force, nor suit can set thee free ;
Until my brother come, I say not when :
Affliction is my name, unloved of men."

I swoon'd, then bursting up in talk deranged,
Shatter'd to tears ; while he stood by unchanged.
I held my peace, my heart with courage burn'd,
And to his cold touch one faint sigh return'd.

Undreamt-of wings he lifted, " For a while
" I vanish.   Never be afraid to smile
Lest I waylay thee : curse me not ; nay, love ;
That I may bring thee tidings from above."

And often since, by day or night, descends
The face obdurate ; now almost a friend's.
O ! quite to Faith ; but Frailty's lips not dare
The word.   To both this angel taught a pray'r.

" Lord God, thy servant, wounded and bereft,
Feels thee upon his right hand and his left :
Hath joy in grief, and still by losing gains ;—
All this is gone, yet all myself remains !"

XXXI.

AUTUMNAL SONNET.

Now Autumn's fire burns slowly along the woods,
And day by day the dead leaves fall and melt,
　And night by night the monitory blast
　Wails in the key-hole, telling how it pass'd
O'er empty fields, or upland solitudes,
　Or grim wide wave; and now the power is felt
Of melancholy, tenderer in its moods
　Than any joy indulgent summer dealt.
Dear friends, together in the glimmering eve,
　Pensive and glad, with tones that recognise
　The soft invisible dew on each one's eyes,
It may be, somewhat thus we shall have leave
　To walk with memory, when distant lies
Poor Earth, where we were wont to live and grieve.

THE MUSIC-MASTER.

A Love Story.

THE MUSIC-MASTER.

A Love Story.

PART I.

I.

MUSIC and Love!—If lovers hear me sing,
  I will for them essay the simple tale,
To hold some fair young listeners in a ring
  With echoes gather'd from an Irish vale,
Where still, methinks, abide my golden years,
Though I not with them,—far discern'd through tears.

II.

When evening fell upon the village street
  And brother fields, reposing hand in hand,
Unlike where flaring cities scorn to meet
  The kiss of dusk that quiets all the land,
'Twas pleasant laziness to loiter by
Houses and cottages, a friendly spy.

G

III.

And hear the frequent fiddle that would glide

    Through jovial mazes of a jig or reel,

Or sink from sob to sob with plaintive slide,

    Or mount the steps of swift exulting zeal ;

For our old village was with music fill'd

Like any grove where thrushes wont to build.

IV.

Mixt with the roar of bellows and of flame,

    Perhaps the reed-voice of a clarionet

From forge's open ruddy shutter came ;

    Or round some hearth were silent people set,

Where the low flute, with plaintive quivering, ran on

Through "Colleen Dhas" or " Hawk of Ballyshannon."

V.

Or pictured on those bygone, shadowy nights

    I see a group of girls at needlework,

Placed round a candle throwing soft half-lights

    On the contrasted faces, and the dark

And fair-hair'd heads, a bunch of human flow'rs;
And many a ditty cheers th' industrious hours.

VI.

Pianoforte's sound from curtain'd pane
  Would join the lofty to the lowly roof
In the sweet links of one harmonious chain;
  And often down the street some Glee's old woof,
"Hope of my heart"—"Ye Shepherds"—"Lightly
      tread,"
Would mesh my steps or wrap me in my bed.

VII.

The most delicious chance, if we should hear,
  Pour'd from our climbing glen's enfoliaged rocks,
At dusk some solitary bugle, clear,
  Remote, and melancholy; echo mocks
The strain delighted, wafting it afar
Up to the threshold of the evening star.

VIII.

And Gerald was our music-master's name;
  Young Gerald White; whose mother, not long wed,

G 2

Only to make him ours by birthright came.

 Her *Requiescat* I have often read,

Where thickest ivy hangs its ancient pall

Over the dumb and desolate abbey wall.

IX.

The father found a music-pupil rare,

 More ready still to learn than he to teach ;

His art no longer was his only care,

 But now young Gerald with it, each for each ;

And with a secret and assiduous joy

The grave musician taught his happy boy.

X.

The boy's whole thought to Music lean'd and sway'd ;

 He heard a minor in the wind at night,

And many a tune the village noises play'd ;

 The thunder roar'd like bands before the might

Of marching armies ; in deep summer calm

The falling brooklet would intone a psalm.

XI.

The Chapel organ-loft, his father's seat,
    Was to the child his earthly paradise;
And that celestial one that used to greet
    His infant dreams, could take no other guise
Than visions of green curtains and gold pipes,
And angels of whom quire-girls were the types.

XII.

Their fresh young voices from the congregation,
    Train'd and combined by simple rules of chant,
And lifted on the harmonious modulation
    Roll'd from the lofty organ, ministrant
To sacred triumph, well might bring a thought
Of angels there,—perhaps themselves it brought.

XIII.

Poor girls the most were : this one had her nest,
    A mountain mavis, in the craggy furze ;
Another in close lane must toil and rest,
    And never cage-bird's song more fine than hers,

Humming at work all through the busy week,
Set free in Sabbath chorus, proud and meek.

XIV.

And when young Gerald might adventure forth
　　Through Music-land,—where hope and memory kiss
And singing fly beyond the bourne of earth,
　　And the whole spirit full of aching bliss
Would follow as the parting shrouds reveal
Glimpses ineffable, but soon conceal,—

XV.

While all the hills, mayhap, and distant plain,
　　Village and brook were shaded, fold on fold,
With the slow dusk, and on the purpling pane
　　Soft twilight barr'd with crimson and with gold
Lent to that simple little house of prayer
A richly solemn, a cathedral air;

XVI.

His symphonies to suit the dying close
　　Suffused it with a voice that could not ask

In vain for tears ; not ask in vain from those
   Who in the dew fulfill'd their pious task,
Kneeling with rosaries beside a grave ;
To whom a heavenly comforting it gave.

XVII.

Thus village years went by.   Day after day
   Flow'd, as a stream unvext with storms or floods
Flows by some islet with a hawthorn grey ;
   Where circling seasons bring a share of buds,
Nests, blossoms, ruddy fruit, and, in their turn,
Of withering leaves and frosty twigs forlorn.

XVIII.

So went the years, that never may abide ;
   Boyhood to manhood, manly prime to age,
Ceaselessly gliding on, as still they glide ;—
   Until the father yields for heritage
(Joyful, yet with a sigh) the master's place
To Gerald—who could higher fortune grace.

XIX.

But the shy youth has yet his hours of leisure :

　　And now, the Spring upon the emerald hills

Dancing with flying clouds, how keen his pleasure,

　　Plunged in deep glens or tracking upland rills,

Till lessening light recal him from his roaming

To breathe his gather'd secrets to the gloaming.

XX.

Spring was around him, and within him too.

　　Delightful season !—life without a spur

Bounds gaily forward, and the heart is new

　　As the green wand fresh budded on a fir ;

And Nature, into jocund chorus waking,

Tempts every young voice to her merry-making.

XXI.

Gerald, high echoing this delightful Spring,

　　Pour'd from his finger-tips electric power

In audible creations swift of wing,

　　Till sunshine glimpsing through an April shower,

And clouds, and delicate glories, and the bound
Of lucid sky came melting into sound.

XXII.

Our ear receives in common with our eye
   One Beauty, flowing through a different gate,
With melody its form, and harmony
   Its hue; one mystic Beauty is the mate
Of Spirit indivisible, one love
Her look, her voice, her memory do move.

XXIII.

Yet sometimes in his playing came a tone
   Not learn'd of sun or shadow, wind or brook,
But thoughts so much his own he dared not own,
   Nor, prizing much, appraise them; dared not look
In fear to lose an image undefined
That brighten'd every vista of his mind.

XXIV.

Two pupils dwelt upon the river-side,
   At Cloonamore, a cottage near the rush

Of narrow'd waters breaking from a wide
    And pond-like smoothness, brimming green and flush
Dark groves; and here for Gerald, truth to say,
His weekly task was more than holiday.

XXV.

A quiet home it was; compact and neat
    As a wren's nest.   A gentle woman's choice
Had built and beautified the green retreat;
    But in her labours might she not rejoice,
Being summon'd to a stiller place of rest;
And spent her last breath in a dear behest.

XXVI.

That was for her two daughters: she had wed
    A plain, rough husband, though a kind and true;
And "Dearest Bernard," from her dying bed
    She whisper'd, "Promise me you'll try to do
For Ann and Milly what was at my heart,
If God had spared me to perform my part."

XXVII.

As well as no abundant purse allow'd,

    Or as the neighbouring village could supply,

The father kept his promise, and was proud

    To see the girls grow up beneath his eye

Two ladies in their culture and their mien;

Though not the less there lay a gulf between.

XXVIII.

A spirit unrefined the elder had,

    An envious eye, a tongue of petty scorn.

That women these may own—how true! how sad!

    And these, though Ann had been a countess born,

Had mark'd her meaner to the dullest sight

Than stands a yellow lily with a white.

XXIX.

White lily,—Milly,—darling little girl!

    I think I see as once I saw her stand;

Her soft hair waving in a single curl

    Behind her ear; a kid licking her hand;

Her fair young face with health and racing warm,

And loose frock blown about her slender form.

XXX.

The dizzy lark, a dot on the white cloud,

   That sprinkles music o'er the vernal breeze,

Was not more gay than Milly's joyous mood;

   The silent lark that starry twilight sees

Cradled among the braird in closest bower,

Not more quiescent than her tranquil hour.

XXXI.

Her mind was open, as a flowery cup

   That gathers richness from the sun and dew,

To knowledge, and as easily drew up

   The wholesome sap of life; unwatch'd it grew,

A lovely blossom in a shady place;

And like her mind, so was her innocent face.

XXXII.

At all times fair, it never look'd so fair

   As when the holy glow of harmonies

Lighted it through ; her spirit as it were

   An azure heav'n outshining at her eyes ;

With Gerald's tenor while the fountain sprung

Of her contralto, fresh and pure and young.

XXXIII.

In years a child when lessons thus began,

   Child is she still, yet nearly woman grown ;

For childhood stays with woman more than man,

   In voice and cheek and mouth, nor these alone ;

And up the sky with no intense revealing

May the great dawn of womanhood come stealing.

XXXIV.

Now must the moon of childhood's trembling white

   Faint in the promise of her flushing heaven ;

Looks are turn'd eastward, where new orient light

   Suffuses all the air with subtle leaven ;

And shadowy mountain-paths begin to show

Their unsuspected windings 'mid the glow.

XXXV.

Her silky locks have ripen'd into brown,
   Her soft blue eyes grown deeper and more shy,
And lightly on her lifted head the crown
   Of queenly maidenhood sits meek and high;
Her frank soul lives in her ingenuous voice,
Most purely tuned to sorrow or rejoice.

XXXVI.

Within the Chapel on a Sunday morn
   She bows her mild head near the altar-rail,
And raises up that mild full voice unworn
   Into the singing;—should a Sunday fail,
There's one would often mark her empty seat,
There's one would find their anthem incomplete.

XXXVII.

Few her companions are, and few her books;
   And in a ruin'd convent's circling shade,
The loveliest of tranquil river-nooks,
   Where trailing birch, fit bow'r for gentle maid,

And feather'd fir-tree half shut out the stream,
She often sits alone to read or dream.

XXXVIII.

Sometimes through leafy lattice she espies
    A flitting figure on the other shore;
But ever past th' enchanted precinct hies
    That wanderer, and where the rapids roar
Through verdured crags, shelters his beating heart,
Foolishly bent to seek, yet stay apart.

XXXIX.

Then Milly can resume her reverie,
    About a real friend, that she could love;
But finds her broken thought is apt to flee
    To what seem other musings: slowly move
The days, and counted days move ever slowest:
Milly! how long ere thy own heart thou knowest?

XL.

Sooner than Gerald his. His path-side birds
    Are scarcely more unconscious or more shrinking.

Yet would he tell his love in simple words
    Did love stand clearly in his simple thinking:
High the discovery, and too high for one
Who counts his life as though not yet begun.

XLI.

For all the rest seem sage and busy men;
    And he alone despised, and justly too,
Or borne with merely;—could he venture then
    To deem this rich inheritance his due?
Slowly the fine and tender soul discerns
Its rareness, and its lofty station learns.

XLII.

And now, 'tis on a royal eventide
    When the ripe month sets glowing earth and air,
And Summer by a stream or thicket-side
    Twists amber honeysuckles in her hair,—
Gerald and Milly meet by trembling chance,
And step for step are moving, in a trance.

XLIII.

Their pathway foliage-curtain'd and moss-grown ;—

Behind the trees the white flood flashing swift,

Through many moist and ferny rocks flung down,

Roars steadily, where sunlights play and shift.

How oft they stop, how long, they nothing know,

Nor how the pulses of the evening go.

XLIV.

Their talk ?—the dappled hyacinthine glade

Lit up in points of blue,—how soft and treble

The kine's deep lowing is by distance made,—

The quail's " twit-wit-wit," like a hopping pebble

Thrown along ice,—the dragonflies, the birds,

The rustling twig,—all noticed in few words.

XLV.

A level pond, inlaid with lucid shadows

Of groves and crannied cliffs and evening sky,

And rural domes of hay, where the green meadows

Slope to embrace its margin peacefully,

H

The slumb'ring river to the rapid draws ;
And here, upon a grassy jut, they pause.

XLVI.

How shy a strength is Love's, that so much fears
   Its darling secret to itself to own !
Their rapt, illimitable mood appears
   A beauteous miracle for each alone ;
Exalted high above all range of hope
By the pure soul's eternity of scope.

XLVII.

Yet in both hearts a prophecy is breathed
   Of how this evening's phantom may arise,
In richer hues than ever sunlight wreathed
   On hill or wood or wave : in brimming eyes
The glowing landscape melts away from each ;
And full their bosoms swell, too full for speech.

XLVIII.

Is it a dream ?   The countless happy stars
   Stand silently into the deepening blue ;

In slow procession all the molten bars
    Of cloud move down; the air is dim with dew;
Eve scatters roses on the shroud of day;
The common world sinks far and far away.

XLIX.

With goodnight kiss the zephyr, half asleep,
    Sinks to its cradle in the dusk of trees,
Where river-chimings tolling sweet and deep
    Make lullaby, and all field-scents that please
The Summer's children float into the gloom
Dream-interwoven in a viewless loom.

L.

Clothed with an earnest paleness, not a blush,
    And with th' angelic gravity of love,
Each lover's face amid the twilight hush
    Is like a saint's whose thoughts are all above
In perfect gratitude for heavenly boon;
And o'er them for a halo comes the moon.

LI.

Thus through the leaves and the dim dewy croft
   They linger homeward.   Flowers around their feet
Bless them, and in the firmament aloft
   Night's silent ardours.   And an hour too fleet,
Though stretching years from all the life before,
Conducts their footsteps to her cottage door.

LII.

Thenceforth they meet more timidly ?—in truth,
   Some lovers might, but all are not the same ;
In the clear ether of their simple youth
   Steady and white ascends the sacred flame.
They do not shrink hereafter ; rather seek
More converse, but with graver voices speak.

LIII.

One theme at last preferred to every other,
   Joying to talk of that mysterious land
Where each enshrines the image of a mother
   Best of all watchers in the guardian band ;

To highest, tenderest thought is freedom given
Amid this unembarrass'd air of Heaven.

LIV.

For when a hymn has wing'd itself away
   On Palestrina's full-resounding chords,
And at the trellis'd window loiter they,
   Deferring their goodnight with happy words,
Almost they know, without a throb of fear,
Of spirits in the twilight standing near.

LV.

And day by day and week by week pass by,
   And Love still poised upon a trembling plume
Floats on the very verge of sovereignty,
   Where ev'n a look may call him to assume
The rich apparel and the shining throne,
And claim two loyal subjects for his own.

LVI.

Wondrous, that first, full, mutual look of love
   Coming ere either looker is aware ;

Unbounded trust, a tenderness above
 All tenderness ; mute music, speechless pray'r
Life's mystery, reality, and might,
Soft-swimming in a single ray of light !

LVII.

O when shall fly this talismanic gleam,
 Which melts like lightning every prison-bar,
Which penetrates the mist with keener beam
 Than flows from sun or moon or any star ?
Love waits ; and like a pebble of the ground
Th' imperial gem lies willing to be found.

LVIII.

One evening, Gerald came before his hour,
 Distrustful of the oft-consulted clock ;
And waits, with no companion, till his flow'r—
 Keeping the time as one of Flora's flock,
Whose shepherdess, the Sunset Star, doth fold
Each in its leaves—he may again behold.

LIX.

Nor thinks it long.   Familiar all, and dear,
  A sanctity pervades the silent room.
Autumnal is the season of the year ;
  A mystic softness and love-weighty gloom
Gather with twilight.   In a dream he lays
His hand on the piano, dreaming plays.

LX.

Most faint and broken sounds at first are stealing
  Into the shadowy stillness ; wild and slow,
Imperfect cadences of captive feeling,
  Gathering its strength, and yet afraid to know
Its chance of freedom,—till on murmuring chords
Th' unguarded thought strays forth in passionate words.

LXI.

Angel of Music ! when our finest speech
  Is all too coarse to give the heart relief,
The inmost fountains lie within thy reach,
  Soother of every joy and every grief ;

And to the stumbling words thou lendest wings
On which aloft th' enfranchised spirit springs.

LXII.

Much love may in not many words be told ;
   And on the sudden love can speak the best.
These mystical melodious buds unfold,
   On every petal showing clear imprest
The name of *Love*.   So Gerald sung and play'd
Unconscious of himself, in twilight shade.

LXIII.

He has not overheard (O might it be !)
   This stifled sobbing at the open door,
Where Milly stands arrested tremblingly
   By that which in an instant tells her more
Than all the dumb months mused of; tells it plain
To joy that cannot comprehend its gain.

LXIV.

One moment, and they shall be face to face,
   Free in the gift of this great confidence,

Wrapt in the throbbing calm of its embrace,
  No more to disunite their spirits thence.
The myrtle crown stoops close to either brow,—
But ah! what alien voice distracts them now?

LXV.

Her sister comes.   And Milly turns away;
  Hurriedly bearing to some quiet spot
Her tears and her full heart, longing to lay
  On a dim pillow cheeks so moist and hot.
When midnight stars between her curtains gleam
Fair Milly sleeps, and dreams a happy dream.

LXVI.

O dream, poor child! beneath the midnight stars;
  O slumber through the kindling of the dawn;
The shadow's on its way; the storm that mars
  The lily even now is hurrying on.
All has been long fulfill'd; yet I could weep
At thought of thee so quietly asleep.

LXVII.

But Gerald, through the night serenely spread,
  Walks quickly home, intoxicate with bliss
Not named and not examined; overhead
  The clustering lights of worlds are full of this
New element; the soft wind's dusky wings
Grow warmer on his cheek, with whisperings.

LXVIII.

And yet to-night he has not seen his Love.
  His Love—in that one word all comfort dwells ;
Reaching from earth to those clear flames above,
  And making common food of miracles.
Kind pulsing Nature, touch of Deity,
Sure thou art full of love, which lovers see !

LXIX.

Most cruel Nature, so unmoved, so hard,
  The while thy children shake with joy or pain !
Thou wilt not forward Love, nor Death retard
  One finger-push, for mortal's dearest gain.

Our Gerald, through the night serenely spread,
Walks quickly home, and finds his father dead.

LXX.

God's awe must be where the last stroke comes down,
    Though but the ending of a weary strife,
Though years on years weigh low the hoary crown,
    Or sickness tenant all the house of life ;
Stupendous ever is the great event,
The frozen form most strangely different !

LXXI.

To Gerald follow'd many doleful days,
    Like wet clouds moving through a sullen sky.
A vast unlook'd-for change the mind dismays,
    And smites its world with instability ;
Rocks appear quaking, towers and treasures vain,
Peace foolish, Joy disgusting, Hope insane.

LXXII.

For even Cloonamore, that image dear,
    Returns to Gerald's mind like its own ghost,

In melancholy garments, drench'd and sere,

   Its joy, its colour, and its welcome lost.

Wanting one token sure to lean upon,

(How almost gain'd !) his happy dream is gone.

LXXIII.

Distracted purposes, a homeless band,

   Throng in his meditation—now he flies

To rest his soul on Milly's cheek and hand,—

   Now he makes outcry on his fantasies

For busy cheats : the lesson not yet learn'd

How Life's true coast from vapour is discern'd.

LXXIV.

Ah me ! 'tis like the tolling of a bell

   To hear it—" Past is past, and gone is gone ;"

With looking back afar to see how well

   We could have 'scaped our losses, and have won

High fortune.   Ever greatest turns on least,

Like Earth's own whirl to atom poles decreased.

LXXV.

For in the gloomiest hour a letter came,
    Shot arrow-like across the Western sea,
Praising the West; its message was the same
    As many a time ere now had languidly
Dropp'd at his feet, but this the rude gale bore
To heart,—Gerald will quit our Irish shore.

LXXVI.

And quit his Love whom he completely loves;
    Who loves him just as much? Nay, downcast youth!
Nay, dear mild maiden!—Surely it behooves
    That somewhere in the day there should be ruth
For innocent blindness? lead, oh, lead them now
One step, but one!—Their fates do not allow.

LXXVII.

The parting scene is brief and frosty dumb.
    The unlike sisters stand alike unmoved;
For Milly's soul is wilder'd, weak, and numb,
    That reft away which seem'd so dearly proved.

While thought and speech she struggles to recover
Her hand is prest—and he is gone for ever.

LXXVIII.

Time speeds : on an October afternoon
  Across the well-known view he looks his last ;
The valley clothed with peace and fruitful boon,
  The chapel where such happy hours were pass'd,
With rainbow-colour'd foliage round its eaves,
And windows all a-glitter through the leaves.

LXXIX.

The cottage-smokes, the river ;—gaze no more,
  Sad heart ! although thou canst not, wouldst not shun
The vision future years will oft restore,
  Whereon the light of many a summer sun,
The stars of many a winter night shall be
Mingled in one strange sighing memory.

END OF PART I.

THE MUSIC-MASTER.

A Love Story.

PART II.

I.

THE shadow Death o'er Time's broad dial creeps
    With never-halting pace from mark to mark,
Blotting the sunshine ; as it coldly sweeps,
    Each living symbol melts into the dark,
And changes to the name of what it was ;—
Shade-measured light, progression proved by loss.

II.

Blithe Spring expanding into Summer's cheer,
    Great Summer ripening into Autumn's glow,
The yellow Autumn and the wasted year,
    And hoary-headed Winter stooping slow
Under the dark arch up again to Spring,
Have five times compass'd their appointed ring.

III.

See once again our village ; with its street
   Dozing in dusty sunshine.   All around
Is silence ; save, for slumber not unmeet,
   Some spinning-wheel's continuous whirring sound
From cottage door, where, stretch'd upon his side,
The moveless dog is basking, drowsy-eyed.

IV.

Each hollyhock within each little wall
   Sleeps in the richness of its crusted blooms ;
Up the hot glass the sluggish blue flies crawl ;
   The heavy bee is humming into rooms
Through open window, like a sturdy rover,
Bringing with him warm scents of thyme and clover.

V.

From little cottage-gardens you almost
   Smell the fruit ripening on the sultry air ;
Opprest to silence, every bird is lost
   In eave and hedgerow ; save that here and there

With twitter swift, the sole unquiet thing,
Shoots the dark lightning of a swallow's wing.

VI.

Yet in this hour of sunny peacefulness
　　One is there whom its influence little calms,
One who now leans in agony to press
　　His throbbing forehead with his throbbing palms,
Now paces quickly up and down within
The narrow parlour of the village inn.

VII.

He thought he could have tranquilly beheld
　　The scene again.　He thought his faithful grief,
Spread level in the soul, could not have swell'd
　　To find once more a passionate relief.
Three years, they now seem hours, have sigh'd their
　　　breath
Since when he heard the tidings of her death.

VIII.

Last evening in the latest dusk he came,
　　A holy pilgrim from a distant land;

I

And objects of familiar face and name,
    As at the move of a miraculous wand,
Rose round his steps ; his bed-room window show'd
His small white birthplace just across the road.

IX.

Yet in that room he could not win repose ;
    The image of the past perplex'd his mind ;
Often he sigh'd and turn'd, and sometimes rose
    To bathe his forehead in the cool night-wind,
And vaguely watch the curtain broad and grey
Lifting anew from the bright scene of day.

X.

When creeping sultry hours from noontide go,
    He rounds the hawthorn hedge's wellknown turn,
Melting in Midsummer its bloomy snow,
    And through the chapel gate.   His heart forlorn
Draws strength and comfort from the pitying shrine
Whereat he bows with reverential sign.

XI.

Behind the chapel, down a sloping hill,
  Circling the ancient abbey's ivied walls
The graveyard sleeps.   A little gurgling rill
  Pour'd through a corner of the ruin, falls
Into a dusky-water'd pond, and lags
With lazy eddies 'mid its yellow flags.

XII.

Across this pool, the hollow banks enfold
  An orchard overrun with rankest grass,
And gnarl'd and mossy apple-trees, as old
  As th' oldest graves almost ; and thither pass
The smooth-worn stepping-stones that give their aid
To many a labourer and milking-maid.

XIII.

And not unfrequently to rustic bound
  On a more solemn errand,—when we see
A suppliant in such universal ground,
  Let all be reverence and sympathy ;

I 2

Assured the life in every real pray'r
Is that which makes our life of life to share.

XIV.

But resting in the sunshine very lone
    Is now each hammock green and wooden cross;
And save the rillet in its cup of stone
    That poppling falls, and whispers through the moss
Down to the quiet pool, no sound is near
To break the stilliness to Gerald's ear.

XV.

The writhen elder spreads its creamy bloom;
    The thicket-tangling, tenderest briar-rose
Kisses to air its exquisite perfume
    In shy luxuriance; leaning foxglove glows
With elvish crimson;—nor all vainly meet
The eye which unobserved they seem to greet.

XVI.

Under the abbey wall he wends his way,
    Admitted through a portal arching deep,

To where no roof excludes the common day ;
    Though some few tombstones in the shadows sleep
Of hoary fibres and a throng of leaves,
Which venerable ivy slowly weaves.

XVII.

First hither comes, in piety of heart,
    Over his mother's, father's grave to bend,
The faithful exile.   Let us stand apart,
    While his sincere and humble pray'rs ascend,
As such devout aspirings do, we trust,
To Him who sow'd them in our breathing dust.

XVIII.

And veil our very thoughts lest they intrude
    (Oh, silent death ! oh, living pain full sore !)
Where lies enwrapt in grassy solitude
    That gentle matron's grave, of Cloonamore,
And on the stone these added words are seen—
" Also, her daughter Milly, aged eighteen."

XIX.

Profound the voiceless aching of the breast,

    When weary life is like a grey dull eve

Emptied of colour, withering and waste

    Around the prostrate soul, too weak to grieve—

Stretch'd far below the tumult and strong cry

Of passion—its lamenting but a sigh.

XX.

Grief's mystery desire not to disperse,

    Nor wish the secret of the world outspoken ;

'Tis not a toy, this vital Universe,

    That thus its inner caskets may be broken.

Sorrow and pain, as well as hope and love,

Stretch out of view into the heavens above.

XXI.

Yet, oh ! the cruel coldness of the grave,

    The keen remembrance of the happy past,

The thoughts which are at once tyrant and slave,

    The sudden sense that drives the soul aghast,

The drowning horror, and the speechless strife,
That fain would sink to death or rise to life!

XXII.

As Gerald lifted up his pallid face,
　He grew aware that he was not alone.
Amid the silence of the sacred place
　Another form was stooping o'er the stone ;
A greyhair'd woman's.　When she met his eyes
She shriek'd aloud in her extreme surprise.

XXIII.

" The Holy Mother keep us day and night !
　And who is this ?—Oh, Master Gerald, dear,
I little thought to ever see this sight !
　Warm to the King above I offer here
My praises for the answer he has sent
To all my pray'rs ; for now I'll die content !"

XXIV.

Then, as if talking to herself, she said,
　" I nursed her when she was a little child.

I smooth'd the pillow of her dying bed.

 And just the way that she had often smiled

When sleeping in her cradle—that same look

Was on her face with the last kiss I took."

XXV.

" 'Twas in the days of March," she said again.

 " And so it is the sweetest blossom dies,

The wrinkled leaf hangs on, though falling fain.

 I thought your hand would close my poor old eyes,

And not that I'd be sitting in the sun

Beside your grave,—the Lord's good will be done!"

XXVI.

Thus incoherently the woman spoke,

 With many interjections full of woe;

And wrapping herself up within her cloak

 Began to rock her body to and fro;

And moaning softly, seem'd to lose all sense

Of outward life in memories so intense.

XXVII.

Till Gerald burst his silence and exclaim'd,

With the most poignant earnestness of tone,

"O nurse, I loved her!—though I never named

The name of love to her, or any one.

'Tis to her grave here——" He could say no more,

But these few words a load of meaning bore.

XXVIII.

Beside the tombstone mute they both remain'd.

At last the woman rose, and coming near,

Said with a tender voice that had regain'd

A tremulous calm, "Then you must surely hear

The whole from first to last, *cushla-ma-chree;*

For God has brought together you and me."

XXIX.

And there she told him all the moving tale,

Broken with many tears and sobs and sighs;

How gentle Milly's health began to fail;

How a sad sweetness grew within her eyes,

And trembled on her mouth, so kind and meek,
And flush'd across her pale and patient cheek.

XXX.

And how about this time her sister Ann
  "Entered Religion,"* and her father's thought
Refused in Milly's face or voice to scan,
  Or once so lively step, the change that wrought ;
Until a sad conviction flew at last,
And with a barb into his bosom pass'd.

XXXI.

Then, with most anxious haste, her dear old nurse
  Was sent for to become her nurse again ;
But still the pretty one grew worse and worse.
  For with a gradual lapsing, free of pain,
And slow removes, that fond eyes would not see,
Crept on the hopeful, hopeless malady.

XXXII.

Spring came, and brought no gift of life to her,
  Of all it lavish'd in the fields and woods.

* Took conventual vows.

Yet she was cheer'd when birds began to stir
  About the shrubbery, and the pale gold buds
Burst on the willows, and with hearty toil
The ploughing teams upturn'd the sluggish soil.

XXXIII.

" 'Twas on a cold March evening, well I mind,"
  The nurse went on, " we sat and watch'd together
The long grey sky ; and then the sun behind
  The clouds shone down, though not like summer
       weather,
On the hills far away. I can't tell why,
But of a sudden I began to cry.

XXXIV.

" I dried my tears before I turn'd to her,
  But then I saw that her eyes too were wet,
And pale her face, and calm without a stir ;
  Whilst on the lighted hills her look was set,
Where strange beyond the cold dark fields they lay,
As if her thoughts, too, journey'd far away.

XXXV.

" After a while she ask'd me to unlock
　　A drawer, and bring a little parcel out.
I knew it was of it she wish'd to talk,
　　But long she held it in her hand in doubt;
And whilst she strove, there came a blush and spread
Her face and neck with a too passing red.

XXXVI.

" At length she put her other hand in mine;
　　' Dear nurse,' she said, ' I'm sure I need not ask
Your promise to fulfil what I design
　　To make my last request, and your last task.
You knew young Master Gerald' (here her speech
Grew plain) ' that used to come here once to teach ?'

XXXVII.

" I said I knew you well; and she went on,—
　　' Then listen : if you ever see him more,
And he should speak of days are past and gone,
　　And of his scholars and his friends before—

Should ask you questions—knowing what you've been
To me,—Oh! could I tell you what I mean!'

XXXVIII.

" But, sir, I understood her meaning well;
    Not from her words so much as from her eyes.
I saw it all; my heart began to swell,
    I took her in my arms with many sighs
And murmurs, and she lean'd upon my neck
Till we both cried our fill without a check.

XXXIX.

" She saw I knew her mind, and bade me give
    Into your hand, if things should so befall,
The parcel;—else, as long as I should live,
    It was to be a secret kept from all,
And say you never wrote, never return'd,
When my last hour drew near, was to be burn'd.

XL.

" I promised to observe her wishes duly;
    But said I hoped in God that she would still

Live many years beyond myself.   And truly
    While she was speaking, like a miracle
Her countenance lost every sickly trace.
Ah, dear ! 'twas setting light was in her face.

XLI.

" She told me she was tired, and went to bed,
    And I sat watching by her until dark,
And then I lit her lamp, and round her head
    Let down the curtains.   'Twas my glad remark
How softly she was breathing, and my mind
Was full of hope and comfort,—we're so blind !

XLII.

" The night wore on, and I had fall'n asleep,
    When about three o'clock I heard a noise
And sprang up quickly.   In the silence deep
    Was some one praying with a calm weak voice ;
Her own voice, though not sounding just the same ;
And in the pray'r I surely heard *your* name.

XLIII.

" Sweet Heaven ! we scarce had time to fetch the priest.

How sadly through the shutters of that room

Crept in the blessed daylight from the east

To us that sat there weeping in the gloom ;

And touch'd the close-shut eyes and peaceful brow,

But brought no fear of her being restless now.

XLIV.

" The wake was quiet.   Noiseless went the hours

Where she was lying stretch'd so still and white ;

And near the bed, a glass with some Spring flowers

From her own little garden.   Day and night

I watch'd, until they took my lamb away,

The child here by the mother's side to lay.

XLV.

" The holy angels make your bed, my dear !

But little call have we to pray for you :

Pray you for him that's left behind you here,

To have his heart consoled with heavenly dew !

And pray too for your poor old nurse, *asthore ;*
Your own true mother scarce could love you more !''

XLVI.

Slow were their feet amongst the many graves,
    Over the stile and up the chapel walk,
Where stood the poplars with their timid leaves
    Hung motionless on every slender stalk.
The air in one hot calm appear'd to lie,
And thunder mutter'd in the heavy sky.

XLVII.

Along the street was heard the laughing sound
    Of boys at play, who knew no thought of death ;
Deliberate-stepping cows, to milking bound,
    Lifted their heads and low'd with fragrant breath ;
The women knitting at their thresholds cast
A look upon our stranger as he pass'd.

XLVIII.

Scarce had the mourners time a roof to gain,
    When, with electric glare and thunder-crash,

Heavy and straight and fierce came down the rain,
  Soaking the white road with its sudden plash,
Driving all folk within-doors at a race,
And making every kennel gush apace.

XLIX.

The storm withdrew as quickly as it came,
  And through the broken clouds a brilliant ray
Glow'd o'er the dripping earth in yellow flame,
  And flush'd the village panes with parting day.
Sudden and full that swimming lustre shone
Into the room where Gerald sat alone.

L.

The door is lock'd, and on the table lies
  The open parcel.   Long he wanted strength
To trust its secrets to his feverish eyes;
  But now the message is convey'd at length;—
A note; a case; and folded with them there
One finest ringlet of brown-auburn hair.

K

LI.

The case holds Milly's portrait—her reflection :

   Lips half apart as though about to speak ;

The frank white brow, young eyes of grave affection,

   Even the pretty seam in the soft cheek :

Swift image of a moment snatch'd from Time,

Fix'd by a sunbeam in eternal prime.

LII.

The note ran thus, " Dear Gerald, near my death,

   I feel that like a Spirit's words are these,

In which I say, that I have perfect faith

   In your true love for me,—as God, who sees

The secrets of all hearts, can see in mine

That fondest truth which sends this feeble sign.

LIII.

" I do not think that he will take away,

   Even in Heaven, this precious earthly love ;

Surely he sends its pure and blissful ray

   Down as a message from the world above.

Perhaps it is the full light drawing near
Which makes the doubting Past at length grow clear.

LIV.

" We might have been so happy !—But His will
    Said no, who orders all things for the best.
O may his power into your soul instil
    A peace like this of which I am possess'd !
And may he bless you, love, for evermore,
And guide you safely to his Heavenly shore !"

LV.

Hard sits the downy pillow to a head
    Aching with memories : and Gerald sought
The mournful paths where happy hours had fled,—
    Pacing through silent labyrinths of thought.
Yet sometimes, in his loneliness of grief,
The richness of the loss came like relief.

LVI.

Minutely he recall'd, with tender pride,
    How one day—which is gone for evermore—

K 2

Among his bunch of wild flowers left aside,

 He found a dark carnation, seen before

In Milly's girdle,—but alas, too dull

To read its crimson cypher in the full !

LVII.

She smiled, the centre of a summer's eve :

 She sung with all her countenance a-glow

In her own room, and he could half believe

 The voice did far-off in the darkness flow :

He saw her stretch'd in a most silent place,

With the calm light of prayer upon her face.

LVIII.

All this night long the water-drops he heard

 Vary their talk of chiming syllables,

Dripping into the butt ; and in the yard

 The ducks gabbling at daylight : till the spells

Of misty sense recall'd a childish illness

When the same noises broke the watching stillness.

LIX.

Wellnigh he hoped that he had sadly dream'd,

And all the interval was but a shade.

But now the slow dawn through his window gleam'd,

And whilst in dear oblivion he was laid,

And Morning rose, parting the vapours dim,

A happy heavenly vision came to him.

LX.

Kind boons of comfort may in dream descend,

Nor wholly vanish in the broad daylight.

— When this our little story hath an end,

That flickers like a dream in woof of night,

Its slender memory may perchance be wrought

Among the tougher threads of waking thought?

LXI.

Thus Gerald came and went.   Till far away,

His coming and his errand were not told.

And years had left behind that sunny day,

Ere some one from the New World to the Old

Brought news of him, in a great Southern town,
Assiduous there, but seeking no renown.

LXII.

After another silent interval,
   The little daily lottery of the post
Gave me a prize ; from one who at the call
   Of " westward ho !" had left our fair green coast,
With comrades eager as himself to press
Into the rough unharrow'd wilderness.

LXIII.

" Through these old forests (thus he wrote) we came
   One sundown to a clearing.   Western light
Burn'd in the pine-tops with a fading flame
   Over untrodden regions, and dusk night
Out of the solemn woods appear'd to rise
To some strange music, full of quivering sighs.

LXIV.

" Such must have been the atmosphere, we thought,
   The visionary light of ancient years,

When Red Man east or west encounter'd nought
   Save bear and squirrel, with their wild compeers.
But other life was now ; and soon we found
The little citadel of this new ground.

LXV.

" The neat log-cabin from its wall of pines
   Look'd out upon a space of corn and grass
Yet thick with stumps ; 'twas eaved with running vines,
   As though among the vanquish'd woods to pass
For something native.   Drawing to its door,
We question'd of the mystic sounds no more.

LXVI.

" They blended with the twilight and the trees,
   At hand, around, above, and far away,
That first it was a voice as of the breeze
   Hymning its vespers in the forest grey ;
But now we heard not airy strains alone,
But human feeling throb in every tone.

LXVII.

" A swelling agony of tearful strife

Being wearied out and hush'd,—from the profound

Arose a music deep as love or life,

That spread into a placid lake of sound,

And took the infinite into its breast,

With Earth and Heaven in one embrace at rest.

LXVIII.

" And then the flute-notes fail'd.   Approaching slow,

Whom found we seated in the threshold shade ?

Gerald,—our Music-Master long ago

In poor old Ireland ! much inquiry made

Along our track for him had proved in vain ;

And here at once we grasp'd his hand again !

LXIX.

" And he received us with the warmth of heart

Our brothers lose not under any sky.

But what was strange, he did not stare or start

As if astonish'd, when, so suddenly,

Long-miss'd familiar faces from the wood
Emerged like ghosts, and at his elbow stood.

LXX.

" Twas like a man who joyfully was greeting
    (So thought I) some not unexpected friends.
And yet he had not known our chance of meeting
    More than had we : but soon he made amends
For lack of wonder, by the dextrous zeal
That put before us no unwelcome meal.

LXXI.

" We gave him all our news, and in return
    He told us how he lived,—a lonely life !
Miles from a neighbour sow'd and reap'd his corn,
    And hardy grew.   One spoke about a wife
To cheer him in that solitary wild,
But Gerald only shook his head and smiled.

LXXII.

" Next dawn, when each one of our little band
    Had on a mighty Walnut carved his name,—

Henceforth a sacred tree, he said, to stand
   'Mid his enlarging bounds,—the moment came
For farewell words.   But long, behind our backs,
We heard the echoes of his swinging axe."

DAY AND NIGHT SONGS.

Second Series.

I.

THE CHOICE.

Now let me choose a native blossom,
   Ere I quit the sunny fields,
Fittest for my Lucy's bosom,
   Hill, or brake, or meadow yields.

Flag or Poppy I'll not gather,
   Briony or Pimpernel;
Scented Thyme or sprouting Heather,
   Though I like them both so well.

Purpling Vetches, crimson Clover,
   Pea-bloom winglets, pied and faint,
Bluebell, Windflow'r, pass them over;
   Sober Mallow, Orchis quaint;

Striped Convolvulus in hedges,
    Columbine, and Mountain-Pink ;
Lilies, floating seen through sedges,
    Violets nestling by the brink ;

Creamy Elder, blue Germander,
    Betony that seeks the shade ;
Nor where Honeysuckles wander,
    May that luscious balm persuade.

Sad Forget-me-not's a token
    Full of partings and mishaps ;
Leave the Foxglove spire unbroken,
    Lest the fairies want for caps.

Crimson Loose-strife, Crowfoot, Pansy,
    Golden Gorse, or golden Broom,
Eyebright cannot fix my fancy,
    Nor the Meadowsweet's perfume.

Azure, scarlet, pink, or pearly,
  Rustic friends in field or grove,—
Each of you I prize full dearly;
  None of you is for my Love!

Wild-Rose! delicately flushing
  All the border of the dale,—
Art thou like a pale cheek blushing,
  Or a red cheek turning pale?

Is it sorrow?   Is it gladness?
  Lover's hopes, or lover's fears?
Or a most delicious sadness,
  Mingled up of smiles and tears?

Come!—no silky leaflet shaken—
  To a breast as pure and fair;
Come! and thoughts more tender waken
  Than thy fragrant spirit there!

II.

ÆOLIAN HARP.

WHAT is it that is gone, we fancied ours?
O what is lost that never may be told?—
We stray all afternoon, and we may grieve
Until the perfect closing of the night.
Listen to us, thou grey Autumnal Eve,
Whose part is silence.   At thy verge the clouds
Are broken into melancholy gold;
The waifs of Autumn and the feeble flow'rs
Glimmer along our woodlands in wet light;
Because within thy deep thou hast the shrouds
Of joy and great adventure, waxing cold,
Which once, or so it seem'd, were full of might.
Some power it was, that lives not with us now,
A thought we had, but could not, could not hold.

O sweetly, swiftly pass'd!—air sings and murmurs;

Green leaves are gathering on the dewy bough:

O sadly, swiftly pass'd!—air sighs and mutters;

Red leaves are dropping on the rainy mould.

Then comes the snow, unfeatured, vast, and white.

O what is gone from us, we fancied ours?

———————

III.

THE PILOT'S PRETTY DAUGHTER.

O'ER western tides the fair Spring Day
    Was smiling back as it withdrew,
And all the harbour, glittering gay,
        Return'd a blithe adieu;
Great clouds above the hills and sea
Kept brilliant watch, and air was free
Where last lark first-born star shall greet,—
When, for the crowning vernal sweet,
Among the slopes and crags I meet
        The Pilot's pretty Daughter.

Round her gentle, happy face,
    Dimpled soft, and freshly fair,
Danced with careless ocean grace
    Locks of auburn hair:

As lightly blew the veering wind,

They touch'd her cheeks, or waved behind,

Unbound, unbraided, and unloop'd;

Or when to tie her shoe she stoop'd,

Below her chin the half-curls droop'd,

      And veil'd the Pilot's Daughter.

Rising, she toss'd them gaily back,

  With gesture infantine and brief,

To fall around as soft a neck

    As the wild-rose's leaf.

Her Sunday frock of lilac shade

(That choicest tint) was neatly made,

And not too long to hide from view

The stout but noway clumsy shoe,

And stocking's smoothly-fitting blue,

      That graced the Pilot's Daughter.

With look, half timid and half droll,

  And then with slightly downcast eyes,

And blush that outward softly stole,—

    Unless it were the skies

Whose sun-ray shifted on her cheek,—
She turn'd when I began to speak;
But 'twas a brightness all her own
That in her firm light step was shown,
And the clear cadence of her tone;
      The Pilot's lovely Daughter!

Were it my lot, (the sudden wish)—
   To hand a pilot's oar and sail,
Or haul the dripping moonlight mesh,
   Spangled with herring-scale;
By dying stars, how sweet 'twould be,
And dawn-blow freshening the sea,
With weary, cheery pull to shore,
To gain my cottage-home once more,
And clasp, before I reach the door,
      My love, the Pilot's Daughter!

This element beside my feet
   Allures, a tepid wine of gold;
One touch, one taste, dispels the cheat,
   'Tis salt and nipping cold:

A fisher's hut, the scene perforce

Of narrow thoughts and manners coarse,

Coarse as the curtains that beseem

With net-festoons the smoky beam,

Would never lodge my favourite dream,

   E'en with my Pilot's Daughter.

To the large riches of the earth,

 Endowing men in their own spite,

The *Poor*, by privilege of birth,

  Stand in the closest right.

Yet not alone the palm grows dull

With clayey delve and watery pull :

And this for me,—or hourly pain.

But could I sink and call it gain ?

Unless a pilot true, 'twere vain

   To wed a Pilot's Daughter.

Lift *her*, perhaps ?—but ah ! I said,

 Much wiser leave such thoughts alone.

So may thy beauty, simple maid,

  Be mine, yet all thy own.

Join'd in my free contented love
With companies of stars above;
Who from their throne of airy steep
Do kiss these ripples as they creep
Across the boundless darkening deep,—
Low voiceful wave! hush soon to sleep
          The gentle Pilot's Daughter!

IV.

TO THE CICADA.

By Meleager.

From the Greek Anthology.

Cicada! drunk with drops of dew,
What musician equals you
In the rural solitude?
On a perch amidst the wood,
Scraping to your heart's desire
Dusky sides with notchy feet,
Shrilling, thrilling, fast and sweet,
Like the music of a lyre.
Dear Cicada! I entreat,
Sing the Dryads something new;
So from thick-embower'd seat
Pan himself may answer you,

Till every inmost glade rejoices
With your loud alternate voices;
And I listen, and forget
All the thorns, the doubts and fears,
Love in lover's heart may set;
Listen, and forget them all.
And so, with music in mine ears,
Where the plane-tree-shadows steep
The ground with coldness, softly fall
Into a noontide sleep.

V.

THE COLD WEDDING.

But three days gone
Her hand was won
By suitor finely skill'd to woo;
And now come we
In pomp to see
The Church's ceremonials due.

The Bride in white
Is clad aright,
Within her carriage closely hid;
No blush to veil—
For too, too pale
The cheek beneath each downcast lid.

White favours rest

On every breast;

And yet methinks we seem not gay.

The church is cold,

The priest is old,—

But who will give the bride away?

Now delver, stand,

With spade in hand,

All mutely to discharge thy trust:

Priest's words sound forth;

They're—" Earth to earth,

" Ashes to ashes, dust to dust."

The groom is Death;

He has no breath;

(The wedding peals, how slow they swing!)

With icy grip

He soon will clip

Her finger with a wormy ring.

A match most fair.

This silent pair,

Now to each other given for ever,

Were lovers long,

Were plighted strong

In oaths and bonds that could not sever.

Ere she was born

That vow was sworn ;

And we must lose into the ground

Her face we knew :

As thither you

And I, and all, are swiftly bound.

This Law of Laws

That still withdraws

Each mortal from all mortal ken—

If 'twere not here ;

Or we saw clear

Instead of dim as now ;—what then ?

This were not Earth, and we not Men.

VI.

ON A FORENOON OF SPRING.

I'M glad I am alive, to see and feel
The full deliciousness of this bright day,
That's like a heart with nothing to conceal;
The young leaves scarcely trembling; the blue-grey
Rimming the cloudless ether far away;
Brairds, hedges, shadows; mountains that reveal
Soft sapphire; this great floor of polish'd steel
Spread out amidst the landmarks of the bay.
I stoop in sunshine to our circling net
From the black gunwale; tend these milky kine
Up their rough path; sit by yon cottage-door
Plying the diligent thread; take wings and soar—
O hark, how with the season's laureate
Joy culminates in song! If such a song were mine!

VII.

THE THREE FLOWERS.

A Pilgrim light for travel bound
    Tript through a gay parterre;
The cool fresh dew was on the ground,
    The lark's song in the air.
One bud, where free of cloud or mist
    Heaven's colour did unfold,
He claim'd with joy and fondly kiss'd,
    And next his heart will hold.
How happy! might the tender thing,
    The blue delightful blossom,
Have kept the sweetness of its Spring,
    Nor wither'd in his bosom!

He strode along through cultured fields,
    By manly contest won,
And bless'd the sylvan bow'r that shields
    From rage of noontide sun;
But spied aloft a rich red bloom,
    And, good or evil hap,
The slippery precipice he clomb
    To set it in his cap.
Then forward, forward proudly flies,
    Too swift and proud for heeding
How leaf by leaf his vaunted prize
    May scatter in the speeding!

Across a moorland crept his way;
    The heather far and near
Steep'd in the solemn sinking day,
    And the sad waning year.
His bent regard descries a flow'r,
    One little cup of snow,
Whose mystic fragrance hath the pow'r
    To bring him kneeling low.

All on the ground he dropt asleep;
    The leaves made haste to hide him.
Above unrolls the starry deep;
    A white flower nods beside him.

———————

VIII.

SONG,

IN THE DUSK.

O WELCOME! friendly stars, one by one, two by two;

 And the voices of the waterfall are toning in the air;

Whilst the wavy landscape-outlines are blurr'd with
  falling dew;

  As my rapture is with sadness, because I may not
   share,

   And double it by sharing it with *thee*.

   —Cloudy fire dies away on the sea.

Now the calm shadowy earth she lies musing like a saint;

 She is wearing for a halo the pure circlet of the moon;

From the mountain breathes the night-wind, steadily,
  though faint;

  As I am softly breathing, "Ah! might some heav'nly
   boon

   Bestow thee, my belov'd one, to my side!"

   —Like a full, happy heart flows the tide.

———————

ST. MARGARET'S EVE.

I BUILT my castle upon the sea-side,
The waves roll so gaily O,
Half on the land and half in the tide,
Love me true!

Within was silk, without was stone,
The waves roll so gaily O,
It lacks a queen, and that alone,
Love me true!

The grey old harper sung to me,
The waves roll so gaily O,
Beware of the damsel of the sea!
Love me true!

M

Saint Margaret's Eve it did befal,
The waves roll so gaily O,
The tide came creeping up the wall,
Love me true !

I open'd my gate ; who there should stand—
The waves roll so gaily O,
But a fair lady, with a cup in her hand,
Love me true !

The cup was gold, and full of wine,
The waves roll so gaily O,
Drink, said the lady, and I will be thine,
Love me true !

Enter my castle, lady fair,
The waves roll so gaily O,
You shall be queen of all that's there,
Love me true !

A grey old harper sung to me,
    The waves roll so gaily O,
Beware of the damsel of the sea!
    Love me true!

In hall he harpeth many a year,
    The waves roll so gaily O,
And we will sit his song to hear,
    Love me true!

I love thee deep, I love thee true,
    The waves roll so gaily O,
But ah! I know not how to woo,
    Love me true!

Down dash'd the cup, with a sudden shock,
    The waves roll so gaily O,
The wine like blood ran over the rock,
    Love me true!

She said no word, but shriek'd aloud,
The waves roll so gaily O,
And vanish'd away from where she stood,
Love me true!

I lock'd and barr'd my castle door,
The waves roll so gaily O,
Three summer days I grieved sore,
Love me true!

For myself a day and night,
The waves roll so gaily O,
And two to moan that lady bright,
Love me true!

———————

X.

AN AUTUMN EVENING.

Now is Queen Autumn's progress through the land;
  And all her sunbrown subjects are astir,
Preparing loyally on every hand
  A golden triumph.   Earth is glad of her.

The regal curtainings of cloud on high,
  And shifting splendours of the vaulted air,
Express a jubilation in the sky,
  That nobly in the festival doth share.

With arching garlands of unfinger'd green,
  And knots of fruit, a bower each highway shows ;
Loud busy Joy is herald on the scene
  To Gratitude, Contentment, and Repose.

Lately, when this good time was at its best,
  One evening found me, with half-wearied pace,
Mounting a hill against the lighted West,
  A cool air softly flowing on my face.

The vast and gorgeous pomp of silent sky
  Embathed a harvest realm in double gold;
Sheaf-tented fields of bloodless victory;
  Stackyards and cottages in leafy fold,

Whence climb'd the blue smoke-pillars.   Grassy hill
  And furrow'd land their graver colourings lent;
And some few rows of corn, ungather'd still,
  Like aged men to earth, their cradle, bent.

While reapers, gleaners, and full carts of grain,
  With undisturbing motion and faint sound
Fed the rich calm, o'er all the sumptuous plain:
  Mountains, imbued with violet, were its bound.

Among the sheaves and hedges of the slope,
    And harvest-people, I descended slowly,
Field after field, and reach'd a pleasant group
    On their own land, who were not strangers wholly.

Here stood the Farmer, sturdy man though grey,
    In sober parley with his second son,
Who had been reaping in the rank all day,
    And now resumed his coat, for work was done.

Two girls, like half-blown roses twin, that breathed
    Fresh innocent joy,—most gentle rustic pair,
Laugh'd with their five-year nephew, as he wreathed
    Red poppies through his younger sister's hair.

Then walking to their farmstead with the rest,—
    The cheerful mother waiting at the door
Had smiles for all, and welcome for the guest,
    And bustling sought the choicest of her store.

The children running to the poor lame boy,
    Whose crutches on the stool beside him leaning,
Seem'd in his book forgot,—with emulous joy
    Bestow'd the handfuls of their flowery gleaning.

O wealthy rustic roof!   O dainty board!
    Kind eyes, frank voices, mirth and sense were there;
Love that went deep, and piety that soar'd;
    The children's kisses and the evening pray'r.

Earth's common pleasures, near the ground like grass,
    Are best of all; nor die although they fade:
Dear, simple household joys, that straightway pass
    The precinct of devotion, undismay'd.

Returning homeward, soften'd, raised, and still'd;
    Celestial peace, that rare, transcendant boon,
Fill'd all my soul, as heav'n and earth were fill'd
    With the warm lustre of the Harvest Moon,

XI

ÆOLIAN HARP.

O PALE green sea,

With long pale purple clouds above—

What lies in me like weight of love?

What dies in me

With utter grief, because there comes no sign

Through the sun-raying West, or on the dim sea-line?

O salted air,

Blown round the rocky headlands chill—

What calls me there from cove and hill?

What falls me fair

From Thee, the first-born of the youthful night?

Or in the waves is coming through the dusk twilight?

O yellow star,

Quivering upon the rippling tide—

Sendest so far to one that sigh'd?

Bendest thou, Star,

Above where shadows of the dead have rest

And constant silence, with a message from the blest?

————

XII.

THE GIRL'S LAMENTATION.

(To an old Irish Tune.)

With grief and mourning I sit to spin;
My Love pass'd by, and he didn't come in;
He passes by me, both day and night,
And carries off my poor heart's delight.

There is a tavern in yonder town,
My Love goes there and he spends a crown,
He takes a strange girl upon his knee,
And never more gives a thought to me.

Says he, " We'll wed without loss of time,
And sure our love's but a little crime;"—
My apron-string now its wearing short,
And my Love he seeks other girls to court.

O with him I'd go if I had my will,
I'd follow him barefoot o'er rock and hill;
I'd never once speak of all my grief
If he'd give me a smile for my heart's relief.

In our wee garden the rose unfolds,
With bachelor's-buttons, and marigolds;
I'll tie no posies for dance or fair,
A willow twig is for me to wear.

For a maid again I can never be,
Till the red rose blooms on the willow tree.
Of such a trouble I heard them tell,
And now I know what it means full well.

As through the long lonesome night I lie,
I'd give the world if I might but cry;
But I mus'n't moan there or raise my voice,
And the tears run down without any noise.

And what, O what will my mother say ?
She'll wish her daughter was in the clay.
My father will curse me to my face ;
The neighbours will know of my black disgrace.

My sister's buried three years, come Lent ;
But sure we made far too much lament.
Beside her grave they still say a prayer—
I wish to God it was I was there !

The Candlemas crosses hang near my bed ;
To look on them puts me much in dread,
They mark the good time that's gone and past:
It's like this year's one will prove the last.

The oldest cross it's a dusty brown,
But the winter winds didn't shake it down ;
The newest cross keeps the colour bright,—
When the straw was reaping my heart was light.

The reapers rose with the blink of morn,
And gaily stook'd up the yellow corn,
To call them home to the field I'd run,
Through the blowing breeze and the summer sun.

When the straw was weaving my heart was glad,
For neither sin nor shame I had,
In the barn where oat-chaff was flying round,
And the thumping flails made a pleasant sound.

Now summer or winter to me it's one ;
But oh ! for a day like the time that's gone.
I'd little care was it storm or shine,
If I had but peace in this heart of mine.

Oh ! light and false is a young man's kiss,
And a foolish girl gives her soul for this.
Oh ! light and short is the young man's blame,
And a helpless girl has the grief and shame.

To the river-bank once I thought to go,

And cast myself in the stream below ;

I thought 'twould carry us far out to sea,

Where they'd never find my poor babe and me.

Sweet Lord, forgive me that wicked mind !

You know I used to be well-inclined.

Oh, take compassion upon my state,

Because my trouble is so very great !

My head turns round with the spinning-wheel,

And a heavy cloud on my eyes I feel.

But the worst of all is at my heart's core ;

For my innocent days will come back no more.

[NOTE. In some parts of Ireland (I have seen it near Bally-shannon and heard of it elsewhere) is a custom of weaving a small cross of straw at Candlemas, which is hung up in the cottage, sometimes over a bed. A new one is added every year, and the old are left till they fall to pieces.]

XIII.

WISHING.

A NURSERY SONG.

Ring-ting! I wish I were a Primrose,
A bright yellow Primrose blowing in the Spring!
The stooping boughs above me,
The wandering bee to love me,
The fern and moss to creep across,
And the Elm-tree for our king!

Nay—stay! I wish I were an Elm-tree,
A great lofty Elm-tree, with green leaves gay!
The winds would set them dancing,
The sun and moonshine glance in,
The Birds would house among the boughs,
And sweetly sing!

O—no! I wish I were a Robin,

A Robin or a little Wren, everywhere to go;

Through forest, field, or garden,

And ask no leave or pardon,

Till Winter comes with icy thumbs

To ruffle up our wing!

Well—tell! Where should I fly to,

Where go to sleep in the dark wood or dell?

Before a day was over,

Home comes the rover,

For Mother's kiss,—sweeter this

Than any other thing!

———————

XIV.

THE SAILOR.

A ROMAIC BALLAD.

Thou that hast a daughter
  For one to woo and wed,
Give her to a husband
  With snow upon his head;
Oh, give her to an old man,
  Though little joy it be,
Before the best young sailor
  That sails upon the sea!

How luckless is the sailor
  When sick and like to die;
He sees no tender mother,
  No sweetheart standing by.

Only the captain speaks to him,—
    Stand up, stand up, young man,
And steer the ship to haven,
    As none beside thee can.

Thou sayst to me, "Stand, stand up;"
    I say to thee, take hold,
Lift me a little from the deck,
    My hands and feet are cold.
And let my head, I pray thee,
    With handkerchiefs be bound;
There, take my love's gold handkerchief,
    And tie it tightly round.

Now bring the chart, the doleful chart;
    See, where these mountains meet—
The clouds are thick around their head,
    The mists around their feet:
Cast anchor here; 'tis deep and safe
    Within the rocky cleft;

The little anchor on the right,
　　The great one on the left.

And now to thee, O captain,
　　Most earnestly I pray,
That they may never bury me
　　In church or cloister gray ;—
But on the windy sea-beach,
　　At the ending of the land,
All on the surfy sea-beach,
　　Deep down into the sand.

For there will come the sailors,
　　Their voices I shall hear,
And at casting of the anchor
　　The yo-ho loud and clear ;
And at hauling of the anchor
　　The yo-ho and the cheer,—
Farewell, my love, for to thy bay
　　I nevermore may steer !

XV.

THE LULLABY.

I saw two children hush'd to death,
  In lap of One with silver wings,
Hearkening a lute, whose latest breath
  Low linger'd on the trembling strings.

Her face is very pale and fair,
  Her hooded eyelids darkly shed
Celestial love, and all her hair
  Is like a crown around her head.

Each ripple sinking in its place,
  Along the lute's faint-ebbing strain,
Seems echo'd slowlier from her face,
  And echo'd back from theirs again.

Yes, now is silence.   Do not weep.
  Her eyes are fix'd: observe them long;
And spell, if thou canst pierce so deep,
  The purpose of a nobler song.

———————

XVI

A MOUNTAIN SONG.

THANK Heav'n, we live in a mountain land!
Where a flight without wings is at our command,—
To sport with the streams in their leaping youth,
Let them swell in spate or dwindle in drouth;
To set o'er the clouds our Olympian seat,
Where the thunder is roll'd beneath our feet,
　　　Where storm and lightning,
　　　And sunshine bright'ning,
Solemnly girdle our steep retreat!

Above, the king-eagle's realm we share,
Below, the haunts of the shy brown hare:
Thousand fields with their lakes a-shine,
Far hamlet and town, and the ocean line,—

Beechen valley, and bilberry dell,
And glen where the Echoes and Fairies dwell,
      With heaps and bosses
        Of plume-fern and mosses,
Scarlet rowan, and slight blue-bell.

The plume-fern grows by the waterfall,
Where the ash-sprays tremble, one and all,
And cool air murmurs, and wild birds call,
And the glowing crag lifts a dizzy wall
To the blue, through green leaves' coronal,
      And sunlights twinkle,
      And insects wrinkle
The deep dark pool of the waterfall.

Watch-towers of morn the mountains rise,
And they treasure the last light of the skies,
Wear shadows at noon, or vapoury shrouds,
And meet in council with mighty clouds;

And at dusk the ascending stars appear

On their pinnacle crags, or the chill moon-sphere

       Crowning only

       Summits lonely,

Guarded with gulphs of blackness drear.

Winter, fierce slave, with mutter and frown

Brings the misty robes and the cold white crown,

Blares the high trumpet of the gale,

And crashes the cymbals of the hail,

Till stung into war by the savage strains

Muster the barbarous suzerains,

       And redly horrent,

       Each roaring torrent

Rages down to the trembling plains!

When pack'd in the hollows the round clouds lie,

And the wild-geese flow changing down the sky

From the salt sea-fringe, then softer rains

Course like young blood through the wither'd veins

That sweeping March left wasted and weak ;
And the grey old Mountain, dim and bleak,
> With sudden rally
> By mound and valley,
Laughs with green light to his baldest peak.

But parched and brown is the heathery husk
When it glows with a judgment-flame through the dusk,
On the dim outline of a huger dome
Than is clad in the paschal blaze of Rome ;
When to river, and valley, and larch-grove spires,
Signal the creeping scarlet fires,
> Keen o'erpowering
> Embers cowering
Low in the west where Day retires.

Your mild blue greeting through distant air
Is the first home-smile to the traveller,
Ye wave in parting his last farewell,—
And he amongst alien fields may tell

Of the haunted lake and the elvish ring,

And the rugged tomb of an ancient king,

      The White Woman mourning,

      The Horse-Fiend* spurning

Your midnight moor on a tempest's wing!

Huge, firm, familiar, mystical range!

Ye guard the child's landscape well from change;

His golden seasons with you abide,

And the joy of song and history's pride;

O, a mountain cradle is loved the best,

From our own hills we reckon our east and west,

      And with fond persistence

      Through time and distance,

Pray in that circle our bones may rest!

---

* Whose Irish name is the *Phooka*. He is supposed to haunt mountainous districts, and to rush or rise suddenly between the legs of the night-traveller, sweeping off with him into the region of inaccessible precipices.

XVII.

MORNING PLUNGE.

I spring from my lightly prest pillow
  To tread the gay sunshiny floor;
O welcome, that glittering billow
  Whose surf almost reaches our door!

The cliff with its cheerful adorning
  Of matted sea-pink under foot,—
The lark gives me " top o' the morning!"
  The sailing-boat nods a salute.

Already, with new sea-born graces,
  Comes many a bright-featured maid,
Peep children's damp hair and fresh faces
  From straw hat's or sun-bonnet's shade.

Green crystal in exquisite tremble,
   My tide-brimming pool I behold;
What shrimps on the sand-patch assemble!
   —I vanish! embraced with pure cold.

A king of the morning-time's treasures,
   To revel in water and air,
Join salmon and gull in their pleasures,
   Then home to our sweet human fare.

There stand the blue cups on white table,
   Rich nugget of gold from the hive,
And there's uncle George and Miss Mabel,
   And Kitty, the best child alive!

Now two little arms round my neck fast,
   A kiss from a laugh I must win,—
You don't deserve one bit of breakfast,
   You unbaptized people within!

XVIII.

THE BIRD.

A NURSERY SONG.

"BIRDIE, Birdie, will you pet?
Summer is far and far away yet.
You'll have silken quilts and a velvet bed,
And a pillow of satin for your head!"

"I'd rather sleep in the ivy wall;
No rain comes through, tho' I hear it fall;
The sun peeps gay at dawn of day,
And I sing, and wing away, away!"

"O Birdie, Birdie, will you pet?
Diamond-stones and amber and jet
We'll string on a necklace fair and fine,
To please this pretty bird of mine!"

" O thanks for diamonds, and thanks for jet,
But here is something daintier yet,—
A feather-necklace round and round,
That I wouldn't sell for a thousand pound !"

" O Birdie, Birdie, wont you pet ?
We'll buy you a dish of silver fret,
A golden cup and an ivory seat,
And carpets soft beneath your feet !"

" Can running water be drunk from gold ?
Can a silver dish the forest hold ?
A rocking twig is the finest chair,
And the softest paths lie through the air,—
Goodbye, goodbye to my lady fair !"

XIX.

A BOY'S BURIAL.

On a sunny Saturday evening
    They laid him in his grave,
      When the sycamore had not a shaking leaf,
        And the harbour not a wave.
The sandhills lay in the yellow ray
Ripe with the sadness of parting May;
Sad were the mountains blue and lone
That keep the landscape as their own;
The rocky slope of the distant fell;
The river issuing from the dell;—
And when had ended the voice of pray'r
The Fall's deep bass was left on the air,
        Rolling down.

Young he was and hopeful,
  And ah, to die so soon!
His new grave lies deserted
  At the rising of the moon;
But when morn comes round, and the church bells
    sound,
The little children may sit on the mound,
And talk of him, and as they talk,
Puff from the dandelion stalk
Its feathery globe, that reckons best
Their light-wing'd hours;—while the town is at rest,
And the stone-chacker rattles here and there,
And the glittering Fall makes a tune in the air,
        Rolling down.

XX.

ON THE SUNNY SHORE.

CHECQUER'D with woven shadows as I lay
    Among the grass, blinking the watery gleam;
I saw an Echo-Spirit in his bay,
    Most idly floating in the noontide beam.
Slow heaved his filmy skiff, and fell, with sway
    Of ocean's giant pulsing, and the Dream,
Buoy'd like the young moon on a level stream
    Of greenish vapour at decline of day,
Swam airily,—watching the distant flocks
    Of sea-gulls, whilst a foot in careless sweep
Touch'd the clear-trembling cool with tiny shocks,
    Faint-circling; till at last he dropt asleep,
Lull'd by the hush-song of the glittering deep
    Lap-lapping drowsily the heated rocks.

———————

XXI.

THE NOBLEMAN'S WEDDING.

(*To an old Irish Tune.*)

ONCE I was guest at a Nobleman's wedding;
   Fair was the Bride, but she scarce had been kind;
And now in our mirth, she had tears nigh the shedding;
   Her former true lover still runs in her mind.

Clothed like a minstrel, her former true lover
   Has taken his harp up, and tuned all the strings;
There among strangers, his grief to discover,
   A fair maiden's falsehood he bitterly sings.

" O here is the token of gold that was broken;
   Through seven long years it was kept for your sake;
You gave it to me as a true lover's token;
   No longer I'll wear it, asleep or awake."

She sat in her place by the head of the table,
 The words of his ditty she mark'd them right well;
To sit any longer this bride was not able,
 So down, in a faint, from the carved chair she fell.

" O one, one request, my lord, one and no other,
 O this one request will you grant it to me?
To lie for this night in the arms of my mother,
 And ever, and ever, thereafter with thee."

Her one one request it was granted her fairly;
 Pale were her cheeks as she went up to bed;
And the very next morning, early, early,
 They rose and they found this young bride was dead.

The bridegroom ran quickly, he held her, he kiss'd her,
 He spoke loud and low, and listen'd full fain;
He call'd on her waiting-maids round to assist her,
 But nothing could bring the lost breath back again.

O carry her softly! the grave is made ready;

   At head and at foot plant a laurel-bush green;

For she was a young and a sweet noble lady,

   The fairest young bride that I ever have seen.

———

XXII.

WOULD I KNEW!

PLAYS a child in a garden fair
    Where the demigods are walking;
Playing unsuspected there
As a bird within the air,
    Listens to their wondrous talking:
"Would I knew—would I knew
What it is they say and do!"

Stands a youth at city-gate,
    Sees the knights go forth together,
Parleying superb, elate,
Pair by pair in princely state,
    Lance and shield and haughty feather:

" Would I knew—would I knew
What it is they say and do!"

Bends a man with trembling knees
 By a gulph of cloudy border;
Deaf, he hears no voice from these
·Winged shades he dimly sees
 Passing by in solemn order:
" Would I knew—O would I knew
What it is they say and do!"

———

XXIII.

BY THE MORNING SEA.

THE wind shakes up the sleepy clouds
　　To kiss the ruddied Morn,
And from their awful misty shrouds
　　The mountains are new-born:
The Sea lies fresh with open eyes;
　　Night-fears and moaning dreams
Brooding like clouds on nether skies,
　　Have sunk below, and beams
Dance on the floor like golden flies,
　　Or strike with joyful gleams
Some white-wing'd ship, a wandering star
Of Ocean, piloting afar.

In brakes, in woods, in cottage-eaves,
    The early birds are rife,
Quick voices thrill the sprinkled leaves
    In ecstasy of life;
And with the gratitude of flowers
    The morning's breath is sweet,
And cool with dew, that freshly showers
    Round wild things' hasty feet.
But the heavenly guests of quiet hours
    To inner skies retreat,
From human thoughts of lower birth
That stir upon the waking earth.

Across a thousand leagues of land
    The mighty Sun looks free,
And in their fringe of rock and sand
    A thousand leagues of sea.
Lo! I, in this majestic room,
    As real as the Sun,
Inherit this day and its doom

Eternally begun.

A world of men the rays illume,

GOD's men, and I am one.

But life that is not pure and bold

Doth tarnish every morning's gold.

XXIV.

THE MAIDS OF ELFEN-MERE.

'Twas when the spinning-room was here,
There came Three Damsels clothed in white,
With their spindles every night;
Two and one, and Three fair Maidens,
Spinning to a pulsing cadence,
Singing songs of Elfen-Mere;
Till the eleventh hour was toll'd,
Then departed through the wold.

    Years ago, and years ago;
    And the tall reeds sigh as the wind doth blow.

Three white Lilies, calm and clear,
And they were loved by every one;
Most of all, the Pastor's Son,
Listening to their gentle singing,
Felt his heart go from him, clinging
Round these Maids of Elfen-Mere;
Sued each night to make them stay,
Sadden'd when they went away.
 Years ago, and years ago;
 And the tall reeds sigh as the wind doth blow.

Hands that shook with love and fear
 Dared put back the village clock,—
Flew the spindle, turn'd the rock,
Flow'd the song with subtle rounding,
Till the false "eleven" was sounding;
Then these Maids of Elfen-Mere
Swiftly, softly, left the room,
Like three doves on snowy plume.
 Years ago, and years ago;
 And the tall reeds sigh as the wind doth blow.

One that night who wander'd near

Heard lamentings by the shore,

Saw at dawn three stains of gore

In the waters fade and dwindle.

Nevermore with song and spindle

Saw we Maids of Elfen-Mere.

The Pastor's Son did pine and die ;

Because true love should never lie.

Years ago, and years ago ;

And the tall reeds sigh as the wind doth blow.

XXV.

A VALENTINE.

Lady fair, lady fair,
    Seated with the scornful,
Though your beauty be so rare,
    I were but a born fool
Still to seek my pleasure there.

To love your features and your hue,
    All your glowing beauty,
All in short that's good of you,
    Was and is my duty,
As to love all beauty too.

But now a fairer face I've got,
 A Picture's—and believe me,
I never look'd to you for what
 A picture cannot give me:
What you've more, improves you not.

Your queenly lips can speak, and prove
 The means of your uncrowning;
Your brow can change, your eyes can move,
 Which grants you power of frowning;
Hers have Heav'n's one thought, of Love.

So now I give good-bye, *ma belle*,
 And lose no great good by it;
You're fair, yet I can smile farewell,
 As you must shortly sigh it,
To your bright, light outer shell!

XXVI

UNDER THE GRASS.

WHERE these green mounds o'erlook the mingling Erne
   And salt Atlantic, clay that walk'd as Man
A thousand years ago, some Vikin stern,
   May rest, or chieftain high of nameless clan;
And when my dusty remnant shall return
   To the great passive World, and nothing can
With eye, or lip, or finger, any more,
O lay it there too, by the river shore.

The silver salmon shooting up the fall,
   Itself at once the arrow and the bow;
The shadow of the old quay's weedy wall
   Cast on the shining turbulence below;
The water-voice which ever seems to call
   Far off out of my childhood's long-ago;

The gentle washing of the harbour wave;
Be these the sights and sounds around my grave.

Soothed also with thy friendly beck, my town,
  And near the square grey tower within whose shade
Was many of my kin's last lying-down;
  Whilst, by the broad heavens changefully array'd,
Empurpling mountains its horizon crown;
  And westward 'tween low hummocks is display'd
In lightsome hours, the level pale blue sea,
With sails upon it creeping silently:

Or, other time, beyond that tawny sand,
  An ocean glooming underneath the shroud
Drawn thick athwart it by tempestuous hand;
  When like a mighty fire the bar roars loud,
As though the whole sea came to whelm the land,—
  The gull flies white against the stormy cloud,
And in the weather-gleam the breakers mark
A ghastly line upon the waters dark.

A green unfading quilt above be spread,
  And freely round let all the breezes blow;
May children play beside the breathless bed,
  Holiday lasses by the cliff-edge go;
And manly games upon the sward be sped,
  And cheerful boats beneath the headland row;
And be the thought, if any rise, of me,
What happy soul might wish that thought to be.

P

XXVII.

NANNY'S SAILOR LAD.

Now fare-you-well! my bonny ship,
   For I am for the shore.
The wave may flow, the breeze may blow,
   They'll carry me no more.

And all as I came walking
   And singing up the sand,
I met a pretty maiden,
   I took her by the hand.

But still she would not raise her head,
   A word she would not speak,
And tears were on her eyelids,
   Dripping down her cheek.

Now grieve you for your father?
   Or husband might it be?
Or is it for a sweetheart
   That's roving on the sea?

It is not for my father,
   I have no husband dear,
But oh! I had a sailor lad
   And he is lost, I fear.

Three long years
   I am grieving for his sake,
And when the stormy wind blows loud,
   I lie all night awake.

I caught her in my arms,
   And she lifted up her eyes,
I kiss'd her ten times over
   In the midst of her surprise.

Cheer up, cheer up, my Nanny,
　　And speak again to me ;
O dry your tears, my darling,
　　For I'll go no more to sea.

I have a love, a true true love,
　　And I have golden store,
The wave may flow, the breeze may blow,
　　They'll carry me no more !

XXVIII.

FROST IN THE HOLIDAYS.

THE time of Frost is the time for me!
When the gay blood spins through the heart with glee,
When the voice leaps out with a chiming sound,
And the footstep rings on the musical ground;
When the earth is white, and the air is bright,
And every breath is a new delight!

While Yesterday sank, full soon, to rest,
What a glorious sky!—through the level west
Pink clouds in a delicate greenish haze,
Which deepen'd up into purple greys,
With stars aloft as the light decreas'd,
Till the great moon rose in the rich blue east.

And Morning!—each pane is a garden of frost,
Of delicate flowering, as quickly lost;
For the stalks are fed by the moon's cold beams,
And the leaves are woven like woof of dreams
By Night's keen breath, and a glance of the Sun
Like dreams will scatter them every one.

Hurra! the lake is a league of glass!
Buckle and strap on the stiff white grass.
Off we shoot, and poise and wheel,
And swiftly turn upon scoring heel;
And our flying sandals chirp and sing
Like a flock of swallows upon the wing.

Away from the crowd with the wind we drift,
No vessel's motion so smoothly swift;
Fainter and fainter the tumult grows,
And the gradual stillness and wide repose
Touch with a hue more soft and grave
The lapse of joy's declining wave.

Here the ice is pure ; a glance may sound
Deep through the awful, dim profound,
To the water dungeons where snake-weeds hide,
Over which, as self-upborne, we glide,
Like wizards on dark adventure bent,
The masters of every element.

Homeward now.　The shimmering snow
Kisses our hot cheeks as we go ;
Wavering down the feeble wind,
Like a manifold Dream to a Poet's mind,
Till the earth, and the trees, and the icy lakes,
Are slowly clothed with the countless flakes.

At home are we by the merry fire,
Ranged in a ring to our heart's desire.
And who is to tell some wondrous tale,
Almost to turn the warm cheeks pale,
Set chin on hands, make grave eyes stare,
Draw slowly nearer each stool and chair ?

The one low voice goes wandering on

In a mystic world, whither all are gone;

The shadows dance; little Caroline

Has stolen her fingers up into mine.

But the night outside is very chill,

And the Frost hums loud at the window-sill.

XXIX.

DEATH DEPOSED.

DEATH stately came to a young man, and said
   "If thou wert dead,
What matter?" The young man replied,
   "See my young bride,
Whose life were all one blackness if I died.
My land requires me; and the world's self, too,
Methinks, would miss some things that I can do."

Then Death in scorn this only said,
   "Be dead."
And so he was. And soon another's hand
   Made rich his land.

The sun, too, of three summers had the might
To bleach the widow's hue, light and more light,
          Again to bridal white.
And nothing seem'd to miss beneath that sun
          His work undone.

But Death soon met another man, whose eye
          Was Nature's spy ;
Who said, " Forbear thy most triumphant scorn.
          The weakest born
Of all the sons of men, is by his birth
An heir of the Eternal Strength ; and Earth
Feels and is movèd by him in his place,
          And wears his trace.

"Thou,—the mock Tyrant that men fear and hate,
          Grim fleshless Fate,
Cold, dark, and wormy thing of loss and tears !
          Not in the sepulchres

Thou dwellest, but in my own crimson'd heart ;

Where while it beats we call thee Life.   Depart !

A name, a shadow, into any gulf,

Out of this world, which is not thine,

        But mine :

    Or stay !—because thou art

        Only Myself."

———————

XXX.

ON THE TWILIGHT POND.

A SHADOWY fringe the fir-trees make,
  Where sunset light hath been;
The liquid thrills to one gold flake,
  And Hesperus is seen;
Our boat and we, not half awake,
  Go drifting down the pond,
While slowly calls the Rail, "Crake-crake,"
  From meadow-flats beyond.

This happy, circling, bounded view
  Embraces us with home;
To far worlds kindling in the blue,
  Our upward thoughts may roam;

Whence, with the veil of scented dew

That makes the earth so sweet,

A touch of astral brightness too,

A peace—which is complete.

LONDON
SAVILL AND EDWARDS, PRINTERS,
CHANDOS STREET.